AGS

Basic English Composition

by
Bonnie L. Walker

AGS®
American Guidance Service, Inc.
Circle Pines, Minnesota 55014-1796
800-328-2560

About the Author

Bonnie L. Walker taught for sixteen years in secondary schools and college. She holds a Ph.D. in curriculum theory and instructional design from the University of Maryland, an M.Ed. in secondary education, and a B.A. in English. She studied psycholinguistics at the University of Illinois Graduate School, and was a curriculum developer at the Model Secondary School for the Deaf at Gallaudet University. She is the author of *Basic English Grammar, Life Skills English,* and numerous workbooks, learning packages, and sound filmstrips in written expression, grammar, and usage. She was a member of Project EduTech, which investigated promising technologies to improve the delivery of special education services. Dr. Walker has written several papers on the applications of personal computers, video technology, and cable television in education. She has been the director for research and development projects funded by the U.S. Department of Education, the U.S. Department of Agriculture, and the Administration on Youth, Children, and Families. Since 1986, Dr. Walker has been president of a research and development company specializing in development of training and educational materials for special populations.

Photo Credits: pp. vi, 72, 130, 240—Superstock; pp. 10, 30, 114, 162, 178, 200, 218—Jim and Mary Whitmer; p. 230—Rob Cage/FPG International; p. 258—Jon Riley/Tony Stone Images

Printed in the United States of America

ISBN 0-7854-0538-0-H (hardcover)

ISBN 0-7854-0539-9-S (softcover)

Product Number 90030 (hardcover)

Product Number 90031 (softcover)

A 0 9 8 7 6

Contents

Chapter

1

Sentences

What kinds of writing will you do today? Maybe you will write a message to a friend. Maybe you will start your report. Maybe you will send a thank-you note to a relative for a gift. No matter what kind of writing you do, you will try to communicate your ideas clearly. After all, your aim is to be understood! Clear communication depends on clear sentences.

In Chapter 1, you will learn how to build clear, correct sentences.

Goals for Learning

▶ To identify the beginning and end of a thought

▶ To capitalize the first word of a sentence

▶ To end a sentence with the correct punctuation mark

Sentence

A group of words containing a subject and a verb and expressing a complete idea.

As a writer and a speaker, you have ideas to communicate. You express each idea in a unit of meaning called a **sentence**.

When you write, you want your readers to understand your ideas. Here are two basic rules for writing sentences.

1. Use a **capital letter** to begin the first word of the sentence. A capital letter tells the reader that a new thought is beginning.

2. End each sentence with an **end punctuation mark**. The mark tells the reader that the thought has ended. Use only a period, a question mark, or an exclamation point to end a sentence. The period is the most common end mark. Never end a sentence with a comma.

Capital letter

The uppercase form of a letter: A, B, C, and so on.

End punctuation mark

A mark that comes at the end of a sentence and tells the reader where the complete idea ends. Here are the three end punctuation marks:

- *period .*
- *question mark ?*
- *exclamation point !*

EXAMPLE

Not clear: do you know my friend Derek Corelli he lives a few blocks away

Clear: Do you know my friend Derek Corelli? He lives a few blocks away.

Get in the habit of reading your sentences aloud. You can hear where the thoughts begin and where they end.

Activity A List the four sentences below on your paper. Add capital letters and end punctuation marks to make them correct.

> in the fall we like to camp in the mountains. we take plenty of food and water We hike on the trails most of the day we are asleep by eight o'clock at night!

Activity B Read the following words. Decide how to turn them into five sentences. List the five sentences on your paper. Make sure to use capital letters and end punctuation marks.

> my neighbor has a garden on the roof she grows tomatoes there she shares them with everyone in the building how do they taste they are delicious

Word Order in Sentences

When you write, think about word order in each sentence. Sometimes you can move the words around without changing the meaning of the sentence.

Read the three example sentences. Notice how they all begin differently. Notice how they all give the same meaning.

EXAMPLES   The day usually warms up by noon.

Usually the day warms up by noon.

By noon the day usually warms up.

Activity C   Rewrite each sentence below. Change the word order. Find a different word in the sentence to put at the beginning. Capitalize the first word in your new sentence.

1) We go to the lake every Sunday.

2) It is too cold for camping now.

3) We decided to hike instead.

4) We walked steadily for three hours.

5) We saw a deer on the way.

6) Quickly it hid from us.

7) We rested twice.

8) We finally reached the end of the trail.

9) It was time to turn back then.

10) We got a lot of exercise that day.

Activity D   Study the example sentences at the top of this page. Then rewrite each of the following sentences in two different ways. First find a different word in the sentence to put at the beginning. Then make a second sentence by moving this word to a new place. Capitalize the first word of each new sentence.

1) They later saw a deer.

2) It stared quietly at them.

3) It then ran back into the woods.

- Before writing a sentence, think about the words that you are going to use.

- Decide which word would be best to put at the beginning. Make sure it begins with a capital letter.

- Remember to put an end punctuation mark at the end of each sentence.

Part A Read the words below. Find five sentences. Rewrite them correctly on your paper. Capitalize the first word in each sentence. End each sentence with the correct end punctuation mark.

sometimes one person can make a big difference have you ever heard of Rosa Parks she changed American history she refused to give up her seat on a bus the civil rights movement began with her brave action

Part B Change the order of the words in each sentence below. Find a different word to put first. Rewrite the sentences on your paper. Remember to capitalize the new first word. Remember to include an end punctuation mark.

1) Mike listens to music every evening.

2) He enjoys rock lately.

3) He sometimes plays the music loudly.

4) His mother usually complains.

5) He turns the music down then.

Always put a punctuation mark at the end of a sentence. It tells the reader where the idea ends. It also helps the reader understand what kind of idea you have written. Here are four rules to learn.

1. Use a period (.) to end a statement.

2. Use a question mark (?) to end a question.

3. Use an exclamation mark (!) to end a sentence that expresses strong feeling.

4. Do not use a comma to end a sentence.

Activity A   Copy each of these sentences on your paper. Capitalize the first word. Add the correct punctuation mark at the end of each sentence.

1) sports are important to Derek

2) he likes to play basketball and soccer

3) he enjoys watching football

4) baseball bores him

5) do you agree with Derek

6) baseball is exciting

7) picture the bases loaded and a power hitter coming to bat

8) what happens next

9) the hitter strikes out

10) there are plenty of surprises in baseball

Activity B   The paragraph below has eight sentences. List them on your paper. Capitalize the first word of each sentence. Add the correct end punctuation.

> When Derek was a junior in high school, he met Amanda and Laura they liked him very much he liked them also Derek was in good physical shape the girls shared Derek's interest in physical fitness they wanted to improve their fitness the girls and Derek decided to work on their fitness together in six months Derek, Amanda, and Laura all looked and felt much better

Activity C   Read more about Derek, Amanda, and Laura. Notice the details that describe the kind of person Derek is.

> Before he met Amanda and Laura, Derek was shy. He spent most of his time alone running and working out or studying.
>
> Amanda and Laura were very friendly. They decided to become friends with Derek. The girls and Derek hit it off from the start.
>
> Soon Derek, Amanda, and Laura became good friends. They were always together. After a few months, Derek spent less time alone. He had lots of friends, too. He became very popular.

Read each question about Derek. Answer each question on your paper. Use complete sentences. Begin each sentence with a capital letter. Add the correct mark of end punctuation.

1) What was Derek like before he met Amanda and Laura?

2) What did Derek do with most of his time before he met Amanda and Laura?

3) How was Derek different after he met the girls?

4) Why did Derek change?

- Use an end punctuation mark to show your readers where your idea ends.
- Use *only* a period, a question mark, or an exclamation point to end a sentence.
- Do not end a sentence with a comma.

Part A   Read the words below. Find five sentences. Rewrite them in a list on your paper. Capitalize the first word of each sentence. End each sentence with the correct punctuation mark.

> Derek has a job at a gas station he likes to work with his hands is he thinking about becoming a mechanic he has not decided on a career his main interest is sports right now

Part B   Follow these directions.

1) Select a topic from the list below.

- Driving a car
- Riding a bicycle
- Listening to music
- Playing basketball
- Wearing the right clothes

2) Write five questions about the topic you chose. End each question with a question mark.

3) Then write the answers to your five questions. End each answer with a period.

4) Check your work to make sure that each sentence is a complete thought. Make sure that every sentence begins with a capital letter.

Part A Answer each question by writing a complete sentence. Capitalize the first word. Put a punctuation mark at the end.

1) What is a sentence?

2) What are the names of the three end punctuation marks?

3) What is the most common end punctuation mark?

4) Why must a sentence begin with a capital letter?

5) How can writers make their sentences better?

Part B Before you write a sentence, you must have an idea. Only you know the beginning and ending of each idea. Follow these directions.

1) Write five sentences.

2) Tell about something you know. You may write about your neighborhood or your friends. You may write about a game, a sport, or a hobby.

3) Put your sentences in a list. Number them from 1 to 5.

4) Check to make sure each sentence begins with a capital letter.

5) Make sure the sentence ends with the correct punctuation mark.

Part C Find two sentences in each group of words below. Write the two sentences with correct capitalization and end punctuation.

1) my grandfather spent a week at the lake he learned to swim

2) the moon was full last week what makes it seem smaller tonight

3) our class is going to the art museum will you join us

4) this biography tells about Eleanor Roosevelt she led an amazing life

5) what is the most important invention of the twentieth century I believe it is the computer

Part D Change the order of the words in each sentence below. Find a different word to put first. Rewrite the sentences on your paper. Remember to capitalize the new first word. Remember to include an end punctuation mark.

1) William listens to the radio every night.

2) He discovered a jazz station last year.

3) Jazz was new to him then.

4) He is fascinated by jazz now.

5) He bought a ticket this week for a Jazz Greats concert.

Test Taking Tip After you have completed a test, reread each question and answer. Ask yourself: Have I answered the question that was asked? Have I answered it completely?

Chapter

2

Punctuating Sentences

How can you tell that someone is asking you a question? The speaker's voice usually ends with a rising tone. How can you tell that someone is giving an order? The speaker's voice has a firm tone. In speech, changes in tone are clues to meaning.

When you write, you want your words to "speak" from the page. How can you help readers to hear how the words sound? Use punctuation marks in your sentences.

In Chapter 2, you will learn how to punctuate your sentences so that readers will hear exactly what you mean.

Goals for Learning

▶ To recognize the purpose of a sentence

▶ To end each sentence with the correct punctuation mark

▶ To punctuate dialogue correctly

▶ To distinguish direct and indirect quotations

Command
A sentence that tells or orders someone to do something.

Exclamation
An expression of strong feeling.

Question
A sentence that asks for information.

Request
A mild command. It politely tells someone to do something. It often includes the word please.

Statement
A sentence that expresses a fact or gives information.

A sentence has one of four main purposes. The purpose of the sentence determines the end punctuation.

1. Purpose: to make a **statement**
A statement expresses a fact or gives information. A statement is also called a declarative sentence. A statement ends with a period.

EXAMPLES	I am hungry.
	The United States is a democracy.

2. Purpose: to ask a **question**
A question is a sentence that asks for information. A question is also called an interrogative sentence. A question ends with a question mark.

EXAMPLES	Are you hungry?
	What is a democracy?

3. Purpose: to give a **command** or make a **request**
A command tells or orders someone to do something. A request politely asks someone to do something. It often includes the word *please*. A command or request is also called an imperative sentence. A command or request usually ends with a period.

EXAMPLES	Eat this sandwich if you are hungry.
	Please register to vote.

4. Purpose: to make an **exclamation**
An exclamatory sentence expresses strong feeling. It may make a statement or give a strong command. It ends with an exclamation point.

EXAMPLES	I'm really hungry!
	Vote today!

Activity A Read the following conversation between Derek and Amanda. Write the purpose of each sentence on your paper. Choose from these four purposes:

- to make a statement
- to ask a question
- to give a command or make a request
- to express strong feeling

1) Amanda: What do you think of Mr. Lamar's music class?

2) Derek: I like the old recordings.

3) Amanda: Tell me more.

4) Derek: I wish I could have heard Robert Johnson.

5) Amanda: Wasn't he a blues musician?

6) Derek: He was the greatest!

7) Amanda: That music sounds old-fashioned to me.

8) Derek: Give it another chance.

Activity B Read the following conversation between Amanda and Laura. The end punctuation is missing. Copy each sentence on your paper. Add the end punctuation that matches the purpose of the sentence.

1) Laura: Are you as hungry as I am

2) Amanda: I'm starving

3) Laura: Is it lunchtime yet

4) Amanda: Look at your watch

5) Laura: It's only ten o'clock

6) Amanda: I need a snack

7) Laura: I have an apple

8) Amanda: Please cut it in half

Punctuation: Questions and Answers

Always put a question mark after a question. An answer is a statement. Use a period at the end of an answer. Study the punctuation in the examples below.

> **EXAMPLES**
>
> Question: When did John F. Kennedy become president of the United States?
>
> Answer: John F. Kennedy became president in 1961.
>
> Question: Who invented the telephone?
>
> Answer: Alexander Graham Bell invented the telephone.

Activity C   Rewrite the following questions and answers. Some of these sentences begin with a capital letter and end with the correct mark of end punctuation. Other sentences have errors. Find and correct any mistakes.

1) What is your favorite dessert.

2) i like chocolate ice cream.

3) Have you ever eaten chocolate mousse?

4) No, I haven't?

5) What is chocolate mousse.

6) Chocolate mousse is a chilled dessert.

7) it is very sweet, very filling, and very delicious.

8) I do not think that I should try mousse?

9) Why not.

10) I am determined to stay away from sweets,

Activity D   Write five questions about famous people. Write the answer to each question. Check to be sure each sentence starts with a capital letter and ends with the correct punctuation mark.

Punctuation: Exclamations

Say the following sentences aloud. Listen for the difference in tone. The words are the same, but the sentence with the exclamation point has the stronger feeling. Remember that most sentences end with a period. Use an exclamation point only when you want extra power.

EXAMPLES		
Statement:	It is late.
Exclamation:	It is late!
Statement:	Arnold looks good.
Exclamation:	Arnold looks good!
Command:	Write to me.
Exclamation:	Write to me!

Activity E   Copy the following sentences on your paper. End the sentence with an exclamation point if it shows strong feeling. If it does not show strong feeling, end the sentence with a period.

1) Amanda is learning to drive

2) Her mother used to race cars

3) Amanda's mother is a great driver

4) Amanda took a lesson from her mother

5) One lesson was enough

6) Watch out

7) Pay attention

8) You're going too fast

9) Amanda signed up at Patience Driving School

10) The instructor is very calm

Here are four main purposes for saying or writing a sentence:

- To make a statement
- To ask a question
- To request or command
- To show strong feeling

Part A Read each sentence below. The end punctuation mark is missing. Decide on the main purpose of the sentence. Number your paper from 1 to 10. Write the purpose of each sentence. Then write the punctuation mark that belongs at the end.

1) Did Ms. Ruiz assign books to read
2) Derek chose a biography
3) What is a biography
4) It tells the story of someone's life
5) Derek's book is about Arthur Ashe
6) Wasn't he a tennis player
7) That's not all
8) Ashe was a true hero
9) What book will you choose
10) I think I'll read a biography

Part B Write ten sentences on your paper. Include three statements, three questions, two commands or requests, and two exclamations. Be sure to use the correct punctuation mark at the end of each sentence.

Dialogue is conversation. The speaker's exact words are called a **quotation**. This lesson has eleven rules for writing dialogue.

Dialogue

The words that people or story characters say to each other.

1. Put quotation marks around a speaker's exact words.

> **EXAMPLE**   "Where are you going?" asked Amanda.

Quotation

A passage containing someone's exact spoken or written words. The words are enclosed in quotation marks (" ").

2. Capitalize the first word of a quotation.

> **EXAMPLE**   Laura answered, "Now I'm going to lunch."

3. You may name the speaker before the quotation. Then use a comma before the quotation.

> **EXAMPLE**   Amanda said, "I will see you later."

4. You may name the speaker after the quotation. If the quotation is a statement, use a comma (not a period) to separate the speaker's name from the quotation. Set the comma inside the closing quotation marks.

> **EXAMPLE**   "I'll see you at the bus stop," said Laura.

5. If the quotation is a question, use a question mark at the end of the quotation. If the speaker's sentence expresses strong feeling, use an exclamation point.

> **EXAMPLES**   "Will you be on time?" asked Amanda.
> "Of course, I will!" said Laura.

Activity A   Rewrite these sentences. Punctuate them correctly.

1) I am going to Centerville said Laura.
2) Why are you going there asked Amanda.
3) I want to see a rodeo answered Laura.
4) Take me with you said Amanda.
5) Sure, come along replied Laura.

6. The whole sentence must end with the correct end punctuation mark. Study the end punctuation marks used in the examples. The first example is a statement; it ends with a period. The second example is a question; it ends with a question mark.

> **EXAMPLES** "We are leaving for Centerville tomorrow."
> Amanda asked, "How long will we be there?"

7. The punctuation mark at the end of the quotation goes inside the closing quotation marks.

> **EXAMPLES** "I want to see the steer wrestling!"
> "I want to see the broncs," said Laura.
> "I am looking forward to seeing my first rodeo."

Activity B Check your knowledge of writing dialogue. Rewrite the following sentences. Punctuate them correctly. Follow the rules and examples given on pages 17–18.

1) How far are we from Centerville asked Amanda.

2) About two hundred miles said Laura.

3) Amanda asked when does the rodeo begin

4) The rodeo begins at noon Laura answered

5) I am getting excited Amanda said with a laugh

6) The first event is the steer wrestling Laura said

7) Then Amanda said I can hardly believe that we will soon be there.

8) I have never seen a rodeo added Laura.

9) Neither have I commented Amanda.

10) Do you think that you will like the rodeo asked Laura.

11) I know I will said Amanda.

8. Start a new paragraph with each new speaker. Study the examples.

"Here we are at last!" said Laura.

"I am pleased to be in Centerville to see a rodeo," said Amanda.

"Me, too!" added Laura.

9. You may want the speaker to say several sentences. Use quotation marks only at the beginning and at the end of the entire speech. Study the example.

"Just think, only yesterday we were back home in Springfield. Now we are in Centerville. Soon we will be seeing a rodeo," Amanda said to Laura.

Activity C   Review the rules for writing dialogue given on pages 17–19. Then read the following sentences carefully. Each of these quotations is incorrect. Find the errors. Then rewrite each sentence on your paper. Make the necessary corrections.

1) "let's buy a postcard for Derek," suggested Amanda.

2) "Which card do you like best," asked Laura.

3) I like them all, "said Amanda."

4) Laura added. "Let's buy one of each."

5) That's a good idea, Amanda agreed.

6) "We can put some in our scrapbooks," Laura suggested

7) "Now let's go to the rodeo," "The show is about to begin," Amanda said.

8) "I hope we have good seats," Laura said. "I would like to be in the front row," Amanda added.

10. You may want to interrupt a one-sentence quotation with words that identify the speaker. In an interrupted quotation, the second part begins with a lowercase letter.

EXAMPLES

"Maybe we'll see the bronc riding first," said Amanda, "or the calf roping."

"We want to see every event," she added, "if we can stay long enough."

11. Do not capitalize the first word of the words identifying the speaker unless it is a person's name. Compare the following examples. *Amanda* is capitalized, but *she* is not.

EXAMPLES

"Here comes a bull rider," **Amanda** shouted.

"There are the rodeo clowns," she added.

Activity D   Review all the rules for writing dialogue on pages 17–20. Then read the following dialogue carefully. Notice that it has no punctuation and no capitalization. Rewrite the entire dialogue on your paper. Add the correct punctuation and capitalization.

Hint: There may be more than one sentence in each numbered item.

1) there are ten riders in this contest Amanda said which one will win

2) the first rider will be Rudy Mendez said the announcer

3) Laura called out come on, Rudy

4) that was a great ride Amanda said

5) give Rudy a big cheer said the announcer

6) how long did Rudy stay on asked Laura did you hear the count

7) Amanda said he must have been on close to eight seconds

Words of Direct Address

When you are writing a letter or a message, you may want to name the person you are addressing. Use commas to set off the name or words from the rest of the sentence. Study these examples.

> **EXAMPLES**
> Joel, thank you for the gift.
> (The sentence begins with the name of the person being addressed. Use one comma.)
>
> Thank you for the gift, my friend.
> (The sentence ends with words that name the person being addressed. Use one comma.)
>
> Thank you, Joel, for being such a good friend.
> (The name is in the middle of the sentence. Use two commas.)

When you write dialogue, you will use words of direct address more often. Use commas to set off the name of or words identifying the person being spoken to. Study these examples.

> **EXAMPLES**
> "Look over there, Laura, at that clown," said Amanda.
> (The speaker is Amanda. She is addressing Laura.)
>
> "Amanda, I don't see the clown."
> (Amanda is being addressed. The speaker must be Laura.)
>
> Amanda said, "Laura, he's letting the bull chase him."
> (The speaker is Amanda. She is addressing Laura.)

Activity E   Copy these sentences on your paper. Add quotation marks and punctuation. Make sure to use commas to set off words of direct address.

1) What is the next event Amanda
2) Amanda said I'm not sure Laura so let's ask someone
3) Excuse me sir what is the next event Laura asked
4) Laura said That man told me the bronc riding is next Amanda

Direct and Indirect Quotations

In this lesson, you have been writing **direct quotations**. You have used quotation marks to enclose a speaker's exact words. You may also tell about conversations with **indirect quotations**. When you write indirect quotations, you do not need quotation marks. The word *that* often appears in indirect quotations.

Look at these examples to compare direct and indirect quotations.

EXAMPLES Direct quotation: "I had a good time," said Amanda.

Indirect quotation: Amanda said that she had a good time.

Activity F Read the following sentences carefully. Identify each sentence as either a direct quotation or an indirect quotation. Write *Direct* or *Indirect* on your paper.

1) "Do you come to the rodeo often?" Laura asked the woman sitting next to them.

2) "Yes, I enjoy rodeos," answered the woman.

3) The woman added that she lived nearby.

4) "Do you live in Centerville?" she asked Amanda and Laura.

5) Laura explained that she and Amanda lived in Springfield.

6) Amanda told the woman, "This is my first rodeo."

7) "Mine, too!" added Laura.

8) Amanda said that she couldn't wait to tell their friends all about the rodeo.

9) "It was so exciting!" she said.

Activity G   Study the examples of direct and indirect quotations on page 22. Then change each of these indirect quotations to a direct quotation. Write the direct quotations on your paper. Punctuate and capitalize each sentence correctly. Remember to use quotation marks. If necessary, review the rules for writing dialogue on pages 17–20.

1) Laura said that she enjoyed the rodeo.

2) Their new friend said that she hoped the girls would come again.

3) Amanda told her that they would definitely come back.

4) Laura said that she liked the bull riding best.

5) The woman said that she liked the bull riding, too.

6) Amanda decided that she still liked calf roping better.

7) The woman wondered how they had heard about the rodeo in Centerville.

8) Laura explained that she had read about it in the newspaper.

Activity H   Rewrite these direct quotations as indirect quotations. Review the examples on page 22. Remember that indirect quotations do not use quotation marks.

1) "Next time let's bring Derek," Amanda said.

2) Laura agreed, "He would enjoy the rodeo."

3) "Who is Derek?" the woman asked.

4) "He is a friend of ours from school," Amanda told her.

5) The woman said, "Be sure to bring him when you come again."

6) "When is the next rodeo?" asked Laura.

7) The woman said, "We have a rodeo every Saturday for the next three weeks."

8) "We'll try to come again someday," Amanda said.

9) "Maybe Derek can come with us the next time," added Laura.

Use dialogue to show what your characters say.

- Put quotation marks around a speaker's exact words.
- Capitalize the first word of a quotation.
- If you name the speaker first, use a comma before the quotation.
- If you name the speaker after the quotation, use a comma after the quotation. Set the comma inside the closing quotation marks.
- If the quotation is a question, use a question mark at the end of the quotation. If the speaker's sentence expresses strong feeling, use an exclamation point.
- Use the correct end punctuation mark at the end of the whole sentence.
- Place the punctuation mark at the end of the quotation inside the closing quotation marks.
- Start a new paragraph with each new speaker.
- Use quotation marks only at the beginning and at the end of a character's entire speech.
- If you interrupt a one-sentence quotation, begin the second part with a lowercase letter.
- Do not capitalize the first word of the speaker identification unless it is a person's name.
- Use commas to set off words of direct address.

Lesson Review   When you write dialogue, use quotation marks around the exact words that someone says. Find the mistake in each of the items below. Then write the sentences correctly on your paper.

1) "Wasn't the rodeo exciting?" Laura asked. "Yes, I'm glad we came," answered Amanda.
2) "I have a paper in English due on Monday, Laura said."
3) The teacher said, "that we could write about anything we wanted," Laura added.
4) "You could describe the woman we met", suggested Amanda.
5) Laura said. "That's a good idea!"

You write sentences for many reasons. You may want to give information or directions. You may want to express your feelings. You may want to ask for information. You may use sentences to tell a story.

Activity A   Some sentences give information. Read these statements that Derek wrote about himself. Notice that no two sentences begin with the same word. Every sentence begins with a capital letter. Every sentence ends with a period.

a) Right now I am a high school student.
b) My hobby is collecting sports cards.
c) I live with my family in an apartment.
d) People say that my brown eyes sparkle.
e) Someday I want to be a diesel mechanic.
f) In the winter I like to ski and ice skate.

Study Derek's sentences. Then write at least six sentences about yourself on your paper. Start each sentence with a different word. Begin each sentence with a capital letter. Punctuate each sentence correctly.

Activity B   Some sentences express feelings. Read the topics below. Choose one topic. Write five sentences about this topic. List your sentences on your paper. Begin each sentence with a capital letter. End each sentence with the correct punctuation mark.

- How I feel on a rainy day
- How I feel about the future
- The best day of my life
- The kindest person I have ever known

Activity C   Some sentences give directions. These sentences are written as commands. Choose one of the topics below. Tell someone how to get from the first place to the second. Use an atlas or a map if necessary.

- Directions from your house to the nearest food store
- Directions from school to your house
- Directions from your classroom to the school library
- Directions from your town or city to the state capital

Activity D   Some sentences ask for information. These sentences are written as questions. Such sentences end with a question mark. Choose a topic that you know something about. Here are some possible topics:

- Your favorite book, movie, or television show
- Your favorite sport or team
- A famous person you would like to meet
- Your town or your school
- An occupation

1) Make up a quiz about your topic. Write five questions that ask for information. Punctuate each question correctly.

2) On another piece of paper, write the answers to your five questions. Punctuate each sentence correctly.

Activity E   Some sentences tell a story. A story often includes dialogue. Read the story given in the sentences below.

a) One day Amanda's dog ran away.

b) Amanda and Laura walked all over the neighborhood.

c) Night came, and it began to rain.

d) The girls came home.

e) "We'll probably never see Benjy again," Amanda said.

f) Suddenly they heard a scratching at the door.

g) "It must be Benjy!" they cried.

h) A wet, tired dog was at the door.

i) Amanda bent down and hugged the soggy dog.

Write your own brief story. List as many sentences as necessary to tell your story. Capitalize all names and the first word of each sentence. Punctuate all sentences correctly.

Be sure to include some dialogue! Remember to include quotation marks around any direct quotations.

You may write sentences for different purposes. Some sentences give information. Other sentences give directions, express feelings, or tell a story. Questions, or interrogative sentences, ask for information.

Part A Match each sentence purpose in Column A with a sentence in Column B. Write the correct letter on your paper.

Column A

1) To express feelings
2) To give directions
3) To ask for information
4) To give information

Column B

a) How do I get to Derek's house?
b) Take the Number 6 bus to get to Derek's house.
c) Amanda's dog is named Benjy.
d) A lost dog brings tears to my eyes.

Part B Follow each direction below.

1) Write two sentences that give information about a place.
2) Write two sentences that could be part of a scary story.
3) Write two sentences that give directions for playing a game.
4) Write two sentences that tell how you feel after a long day.
5) Write two questions to ask about something you have always wanted to know.

Part A Read each of the following pairs of sentences. Find the sentence that has correct punctuation and capitalization. Write the letter of that sentence on your paper.

1) a) Write to tell me how to get to your house.

   b) Write to tell me how to get to your house?

2) a) What a terrific party you gave!

   b) What a terrific party you gave?

3) a) This book tells the life story of a great man!

   b) This book tells the life story of a great man.

4) a) Please send me an application.

   b) Please send me an application?

5) a) Ms. Ruiz clapped wildly. "Bravo!" "Bravo!", she shouted.

   b) Ms. Ruiz clapped wildly. "Bravo! Bravo!" she shouted.

6) a) Blanca sighed, "this has been a hard day."

   b) Blanca sighed, "This has been a hard day."

7) a) "My first job is over," sighed Blanca, "but my next one is about to begin."

   b) "My first job is over," sighed Blanca, "But my next one is about to begin."

8) a) Chantal told Robbie that he looked fine.

   b) Chantal told Robbie that "he looked fine."

9) a) "What is your answer?" Derek, asked Ms. Ruiz.

   b) "What is your answer, Derek?" asked Ms. Ruiz.

10) a) "Hamlet, can't decide what to do," replied Derek.

   b) "Hamlet can't decide what to do," replied Derek.

Part B Change these indirect quotations to direct quotations.
Write the direct quotations on your paper. Capitalize and
punctuate each sentence correctly.

1) Laura told Derek that she had gone to Centerville to see
   a rodeo.
2) Derek asked who had gone with her.
3) Laura told him that she had gone with Amanda.
4) Derek asked if they were going again.
5) He said that he had never seen a rodeo.
6) Amanda told him that she planned to go to the rodeo again.
7) Laura asked Derek if he wanted to go with them.
8) Derek said that the rodeo sounded like fun.
9) He said that he wanted to see the bull riding.
10) Amanda said that Derek would enjoy the rodeo.

Part C Follow each direction.

1) Write a sentence that expresses a fact or gives information.
2) Write a sentence that asks a question.
3) Write a sentence that expresses strong feeling.
4) Write a sentence to request information.
5) Write a sentence that tells someone what to do.
6) Write a sentence that gives a command.
7) Write a direct quotation spoken by a character named
   Alphonse.
8) Write an indirect quotation that tells what a character
   named Claude said.
9) Write a direct quotation in which Alphonse speaks
   to Claude.
10) Write at least two sentences of dialogue between
    two characters.

Test Taking Tip Always read directions more than once. Underline words that
tell *how many* examples or items you must provide.

Writing Correct Sentences

When you write correct sentences, your readers get your message clearly. They are not spending time trying to figure out exactly what you mean. Correctly written sentences also make a good impression. Suppose that two people are writing letters to apply for a job. Person A has written correct sentences. Person B has written sentences with errors. It's easy to see that Person A has the better chance of being called.

Can you recognize common writing mistakes? Do you know how to fix them? In Chapter 3, you will learn how to recognize and to correct six common writing mistakes.

Goals for Learning

▶ To find and correct errors in subject-verb agreement

▶ To find and correct errors in pronoun usage

▶ To recognize proper nouns and proper adjectives

▶ To follow rules of capitalization

▶ To use verb tenses correctly

▶ To use and spell regular and irregular verb forms correctly

▶ To use and spell possessives and plurals correctly

Agreement of Subject and Verb

Agreement
The logical match between two elements of a sentence.

Noun
The name of a person, place, thing, or idea: teacher, museum, ball, heroism.

Plural
Referring to more than one person, place, or thing: houses, nations, doctors, they.

Singular
Referring to one person, place, or thing: house, nation, doctor, it.

Subject
The person, place, or thing that the sentence tells about. Donald ate a sandwich. *(subject: Donald)*

Verb
A word used to express action or state of being. Donald ate a sandwich. *(action verb: ate)* Donald was hungry. *(state-of-being verb: was)*

Each part of a sentence should fit logically with every other part. That logical fit is called **agreement**. Every sentence has a **subject** and a **verb**. The subject of the sentence is the person, place, or thing that the sentence is talking about. Often a subject is a **noun**. The verb tells what the subject is doing. The subject may be **singular** or **plural**.

Study these rules.

1. Singular nouns usually do not end in -*s*. Singular verbs that name present actions usually do end in -*s*.

| EXAMPLES | Sam runs.
| | The wheel squeaks.
| | A dog barks.

2. Plural nouns usually do end in -*s*. Plural verbs that name present actions usually do not end in -*s*.

| EXAMPLES | The boys run.
| | The wheels squeak.
| | Dogs bark.

3. If the subject is singular, the verb must also be singular. If the subject is plural, the verb must also be plural.

| EXAMPLES | Singular subjects and verbs: | The student reads.
| | | A drum booms.
| | | That baby cries.
| | Plural subjects and verbs: | Students read.
| | | Drums boom.
| | | Babies cry.

Activity A Read the following list of nouns. Copy them on your paper in two columns. In the left column, write the singular nouns. In the right column, write the plural nouns. Twelve words belong in each column.

dogs	dress	reports
sentences	movie	dangers
garage	puppies	musician
verbs	teams	fruits
visitors	subject	Derek
box	teacher	science
classes	trees	vacation
cars	dance	weather

Activity B Read the sentences below. Label each bold subject as *Singular* or *Plural*. Write your answers on your paper.

1) The **snow** falls gently.

2) **Knowledge** of rules helps writers.

3) The **answers** pop into my head.

4) My **friends** like music.

5) Those **dancers** whirl like tops.

Activity C Look at the bold subject of each sentence below. Read the verbs in parentheses. On your paper write the verb that agrees with the subject.

1) Sometimes **Benjy** (run, runs) away.

2) That **dog** (jump, jumps) the fence.

3) His **owners** (call, calls) him.

4) The **neighbors** (chase, chases) him.

5) Other **dogs** (bark, barks) at Benjy.

6) Finally the **adventurer** (return, returns).

Singular and Plural Pronouns

The subject of a sentence is not always a singular or plural noun. The subject may be a singular or plural **pronoun** instead. The verb must agree in number with the subject pronoun.

Notice when -s (or -es) is added to the verb *go* and the verb *sing* below. Each verb is made to agree with each pronoun listed.

Singular		Plural	
I go.	I sing.	We go.	We sing.
You go.	You sing.	You go.	You sing.
He goes.	He sings.	They go.	They sing.
She goes.	She sings.		
It goes.	It sings.		

Activity D   Copy each of the pronouns listed below. Use it as the first word of a two-word sentence. The second word of the sentence should be the correct form of the verb *eat*.

1) You

2) They

3) I

4) He

5) She

6) It

7) We

Now write another two-word sentence beginning with each pronoun listed after numbers 1-7. Use the correct form of the verb *talk* as the second word of the sentence.

Some kinds of pronouns refer in a general way to people, places, and things. Some of these pronouns are singular, and some are plural. Others may be either singular or plural, depending on what meaning is intended. Read the examples below.

Singular			
anyone	somebody	neither	no one
anybody	each	everybody	nobody
someone	either	everyone	

EXAMPLE Everybody works. (singular verb: *works*)

Plural			
several	few	many	both

EXAMPLE Both need help. (plural verb: *need*)

Singular or Plural				
all	any	most	none	some

EXAMPLES All go quickly. (plural verb: *go*)
All goes well. (singular verb: *goes*)

Activity E Choose the correct form of the verb to agree with each bold subject. Write your answers on your paper.

1) **Someone** (knock, knocks) at the door.

2) The friends are talking. **Nobody** (hear, hears) the knocks at first.

3) The knocks grow louder. **Several** (make, makes) the door shake.

4) **Everybody** (look, looks) at everybody else.

5) A voice calls out, "Pizza delivery! Two pies here!" **Both** (smell, smells) wonderful!

Verbs With Different Forms

To agree with a singular subject, a verb often ends with -s. Here are two examples:

Verb	Singular	Plural
to know to plan	Jon *knows* he *plans*	the boys *know* they *plan*

Some verbs do not change in a regular way. Their singular and plural forms vary. Their forms vary with different subject pronouns, too. Study these examples of two common verbs with different forms: *be* and *have*.

Verb	Singular	Plural
to be	Jon *is* I *am* you *are* he *is;* she *is;* it *is*	the boys *are* we *are* you *are* they *are*
to have	Jon *has* I *have* you *have* he *has;* she *has;* it *has*	the boys *have* we *have* you *have* they *have*

Activity F   Make each subject and verb agree. Write the correct verb form for each sentence.

1) Derek (have, has) a glass of juice every morning.

2) He (is, am, are) still keeping in shape.

3) After breakfast he (run, runs) a mile.

4) "I (enjoy, enjoys) running," Derek says.

5) "You (have, has) the right attitude!" says Amanda.

6) "I (is, am, are) lifting weights," adds Laura.

7) "We (is, are) all keeping in shape!" says Amanda.

8) "Tell me what you (is, am, are) doing, " says Laura.

9) "I (am, are) taking dance lessons with my mom!"

Finding the Subject

In order to make a verb agree with its subject, you must know what the subject is. Sometimes words come between the subject and the verb in a sentence. Ignore those words. The number of the subject is not changed by any word or words that follow it. Study the examples below.

> **EXAMPLES**
>
> **One** of the girls **knows** Mike.
> (singular subject: *one*; verb: *knows*)
>
> The **rules** in this book **are** important.
> (plural subject: *rules*; verb: *are*)
>
> One **rule** in these books **is** especially important.
> (singular subject: *rule*; verb: *is*)
>
> That **car** often **makes** noise.
> (singular subject: *car*; verb: *makes*)
>
> Those **cars** often **make** noise.
> (plural subject: *cars*; verb: *make*)

Activity G   Find the subject in each of the sentences below. Write the correct form of the verb that agrees with each subject. Remember to ignore any words that come between the subject and the verb in a sentence.

1) The subject of a sentence (is, am, are) either singular or plural.

2) One of Derek's friends (run, runs) thirty miles a week.

3) The girl with red sneakers (dance, dances) well.

4) The actors in the school play (seem, seems) talented.

5) All of the actors (has, have) worked very hard to learn their parts.

6) Neither of the guys (has, have) entered the marathon yet.

7) Both of them (hope, hopes) to do well in their first race.

8) The soccer players on the field (has, have) one ball.

9) The player in the stands (has, have) another ball.

10) Some of the plants (is, am, are) tall.

Compound Subjects

Compound subject

Two subjects joined by and.

Sometimes a sentence has two subjects joined with *and*. A **compound subject** needs a plural verb.

> **EXAMPLES**
>
> Amanda and Laura exercise daily.
> (compound subject: *Amanda, Laura*
> plural verb: *exercise*)
>
> Science and math are Amanda's favorite subjects.
> (compound subject: *science, math*
> plural verb: *are*)

Activity H   Find the subjects in the sentences below. Some subjects are compound. Choose the correct form of the verb to agree with each subject. Write your answers on your paper.

1) Amanda and her mom (like, likes) aerobics.

2) Laura (lift, lifts) weights.

3) She (want, wants) to be a firefighter.

4) Derek and his friend Mike (run, runs).

5) Both Derek and Mike also (play, plays) tennis on the weekends.

6) Golf and bowling (is, am, are) popular sports.

7) Stair climbing (provides, provide) a good workout.

8) Laura and Amanda (swims, swim) at the town pool.

9) Freestyle and the butterfly stroke (is, am, are) Amanda's strengths.

10) The girls (dives, dive) gracefully.

To write correct sentences, make your subjects and verbs agree. Check your understanding of this rule by completing the activities below.

Part A Write the correct form of the verb for each sentence below.

1) The capital of Puerto Rico (is, am, are) San Juan.

2) Laura (likes, like) her Spanish class.

3) Both Laura and Amanda (takes, take) Spanish.

4) "All of us (likes, like) Spanish," they said to Derek.

5) "I (want, wants) Spanish next semester," he said.

6) "Spanish (helps, help) you to learn English."

7) "I (agrees, agree) with that," Derek said.

8) "Everyone (tells, tell) me that learning another language helps me to understand my own," said Amanda.

9) "I (hear, hears) that, too," said Derek.

10) "I (sign, signs) up today!" he said.

Part B Each of these sentences has a mistake. Find each mistake. Rewrite the sentences correctly.

1) Mr. Chang's class and Ms. Ricci's class is preparing a play.

2) One of my friends have a leading part in the play.

3) She play the role of Lady Macbeth.

4) Toward the end, Lady Macbeth lose her mind.

5) "I am made for this role!" my friend say proudly.

A pronoun is a word that is used in place of a noun in a sentence. Pronouns are used to avoid repeating nouns. In each first sentence below, the noun is bold. In each second sentence, the pronoun is bold. Compare each pronoun with the noun it refers to.

The **school** is on Maple Avenue. **It** is an old building.

Have the **students** entered? Have **they** begun their classes?

The **principal** is outside. **She** is waiting for the last bus.

It, they, and *she* are pronouns. Here are other common pronouns:

I	me	our	myself
you	us	his	yourself
we	them	her	herself
he	him	theirs	themselves

When you write, your readers must be able to tell what each of your pronouns refers to. Make sure each pronoun has a clear **antecedent**. The word part *ante* means "before," and the antecedent often comes before the pronoun. A pronoun is near the antecedent, but it is not always in the same sentence.

Antecedent

The noun to which a pronoun refers.

EXAMPLES   Amanda and **Amanda's** mother go to dance class.
Amanda and **her** mother go to dance class.
(*Amanda* is the antecedent for the pronoun *her*.)

The **school** is on Maple Avenue.
It is an old building.
(*School* is the antecedent for the pronoun *it*.)

Activity A   Find the antecedent for the bold pronoun in each sentence below. List each pronoun and its antecedent on your paper. Follow the example.

Example   Does a dog protect **its** human family?
its—dog

1) Derek is studying **his** Spanish lesson.
2) Amanda and Laura enjoy **their** Spanish class.
3) Derek and the girls are helping each other understand **their** Spanish lesson.
4) Derek thought **his** friend Mike would like to take Spanish.
5) The girls enjoy **their** times studying Spanish with Derek.
6) Amanda and Laura enjoyed **their** trip to Texas.
7) Both girls found **their** Spanish useful on the trip.
8) Amanda said, "**I** understood what the names of Texas towns mean because of my Spanish."
9) Derek said that **he** would like to go to Texas with Mike.
10) Mike said they could use **his** car for the trip.

Activity B   Read the sentences below. These sentences are all about the same topic. Find the pronouns and list them on your paper. Beside each pronoun, write its antecedent. There are twelve pronouns in all.

1) Mike said he read about a national park in Kentucky.
2) It is called Mammoth Cave.
3) "I would like to visit Mammoth Cave," said Mike.
4) Derek said to Mike, "Tell me about Mammoth Cave."
5) "It has 144 miles of underground passages," Mike told him.
6) "A river runs underground," he added, "and it is 360 feet below the surface."
7) Derek said, "I wish we could go tomorrow."
8) Mike held up a road map as he said, "Our route is already marked."

Gender
The characteristic of nouns and pronouns that tells they are masculine (man, he), feminine (woman, she), or neuter (puppy, it).

Feminine pronoun
A word that replaces a noun naming a female person. The feminine pronouns are she, her, hers, herself.

Masculine pronoun
A word that replaces a noun naming a male person. The masculine pronouns are he, him, his, himself.

Neuter pronoun
A word that replaces the name of any place, thing, or idea in a sentence. Neuter singular pronouns are it, its, itself.

Gender

Make each pronoun refer clearly to its antecedent. The **gender** of the pronoun should agree with the gender of its antecedent. Study the following rules about using gender.

1. Replace the name of a male person with a **masculine pronoun**.

> EXAMPLE   Harry drives **his** car to work.

2. Replace the name of a female person with a **feminine pronoun**.

> EXAMPLE   The actress played **her** part well.

3. Replace the names of any other singular noun with a **neuter pronoun**.

> EXAMPLE   Our house has a fence around **it**.

4. If the singular noun could be either male or female or both, use the words *his or her*. Since those words can sound stiff, you may prefer to change the noun to a plural.

> EXAMPLE   Each student signed up for **his or her** classes. (singular)
> The students signed up for **their** classes. (plural)

5. Replace plural nouns with plural pronouns such as *they, their, ours,* and *yourselves*. It does not matter whether the group includes males, females, or both.

> EXAMPLE   Ten families came. **They** brought **their** food.

Activity C   Rewrite the following bold nouns as pronouns.

1) Amanda and Laura went to **Amanda and Laura's** Spanish class.
2) Mr. Martin gave **Mr. Martin's** class an assignment.
3) "Did everyone do the assignment?" **Mr. Martin** asked.
4) "**Amanda** did," said Amanda. "Laura has **Laura's** work, too."
5) "My, my! Aren't **Amanda and Laura** wonderful!" Mr. Martin said with a grin.

Number

Make your pronouns agree with their antecedents in **number**. If the antecedent is singular, the pronoun must be singular. If the antecedent is plural, the pronoun must be plural. Study the examples below.

> **EXAMPLES**   Tran liked **the class**. Tran liked **it**. (singular)
>
> Tran liked **the classes**. Tran liked **them**. (plural)

Activity D   Each item below has an error. A pronoun does not agree in number with its antecedent. Find the error. Rewrite the sentences correctly.

1) Springfield shares a recycling center with their neighboring towns.

2) The recycling center is off Main Street. They are located behind the supermarket.

3) Three huge bins are there. It is for glass, newspaper, and plastic.

4) "Trash is a big problem, and landfills are not a way to solve them," said Laura.

5) Amanda agreed, "Each household in town should recycle their trash."

Case

Think about how a pronoun works in a sentence. Then use the correct **case** of the pronoun. A pronoun used as the subject of a sentence should be in the **nominative case**. A pronoun that receives action should be in the **objective case**. A pronoun used to show ownership should be in the **possessive case**.

Examples of each case are shown in the box on the top of the next page.

EXAMPLES	Nominative pronoun:	**She** called Denise.
		Denise and **I** called back.
	Objective pronoun:	Graciela called **her**.
		Denise called Graciela and **me**.
	Possessive pronoun:	Where are **their** phones?
		Are the phones **theirs** or **yours**?

Personal Pronouns				
		Nominative	**Objective**	**Possessive**
Singular	**First person**	I	me	my, mine
	Second person	you	you	your, yours
	Third person	he, she, it	him, her, it	his, her, hers, its
Plural	**First person**	we	us	our, ours
	Second person	you	you	your, yours
	Third person	they	them	their, theirs

Activity E   Study the table above. Then write the personal pronoun on your paper that correctly completes each sentence.

1) Derek had to go to _____ job at the gas station.

2) _____ was a good job, and Derek liked _____ boss.

3) Mabel Lentz owns the station. _____ also liked _____.

4) _____ hired _____ to work part-time.

5) Mabel Lentz started _____ hobby twenty-five years ago.

6) _____ has hundreds of model cars in _____ collection.

7) Derek collects sports cards; _____ show _____ collections to each other.

Using Pronouns and Antecedents

Avoid the error of using a pronoun that has no clear antecedent. Correct the error by changing the pronoun to a noun. Compare these examples:

| **EXAMPLES** | Not clear: | **They** say the Giants will win. |
| | Clear: | **Sportscasters** say the Giants will win. |

Watch out for pronouns that could refer to more than one antecedent. To fix the problem, rewrite the sentence. Or change the pronoun to a noun.

EXAMPLES	Not clear:	Laura told Amanda that she would be late. (Does *she* refer to Laura or to Amanda?)
	Clear:	"You will be late," Laura told Amanda.
	Not clear:	When the dog chases the cat, it always knocks something over. (Does *it* refer to the dog or the cat?)
	Clear:	When the dog chases the cat, the dog always knocks something over.

Activity F   Find the unclear pronoun antecedent in each sentence below. Rewrite the sentence to make it correct. (There is more than one way to correct each sentence. Choose just one way.)

1) Amanda gave Laura her book.

2) They say that California always has great weather.

3) Mike told Derek he would be taking his brother to the game.

4) When Mike plays ball with Derek, he always says he has to go home.

5) It says that prices are going up.

Check your writing for careful use of pronouns. Make sure you can answer yes to each of these questions:

- Does every pronoun have a clear antecedent?
- Does every pronoun agree in number with its antecedent?
- Does every pronoun agree in gender with its antecedent?
- Is the correct case of the pronoun used?

Part A   Rewrite the sentences that Derek wrote about his hobby. Find and correct all the pronoun usage errors.

1) Everyone in my family had their own hobby.
2) My mother gave my sister her stamp collection.
3) Only me had no special interest.
4) My father showed me some old baseball cards him had saved.
5) Them were interesting to look at.
6) So I decided to collect sports cards.
7) A store on Main Street sells it.
8) Ms. Lentz, my boss, has small model cars in their collection.
9) Them are exactly like the full-size cars.
10) Us are both collectors.

Part B   The sentences below tell about the same topic. There is at least one pronoun error in each item. Rewrite the sentences to correct the errors. (There is more than one way to correct the errors. Choose just one way.)

1) They say that birdwatching can be fun.
2) At the park, my friend Derek and me met a birdwatcher.
3) This woman made it sound interesting.
4) She lent Derek and I his binoculars.
5) The two of us saw a cardinal and a bluejay on a tree together. Them colors seemed so bright!

Capitalize the first word of a sentence. Always capitalize the pronoun *I.* Here are other capitalization rules.

Adjective
A word that describes a noun or pronoun. It tells how many, what kind, or which one.

Common noun
The general name of a person, place, thing, or idea. It begins with a lowercase letter: child, playground, swing, happiness.

Proper adjective
A describing word formed from a proper noun: French food.

Proper noun
The name of a particular person, place, thing, or idea. It begins with a capital letter: Frances, Osgood Park, U.S. Senate, Stone Age.

1. Most nouns are **common nouns**. Use a lowercase letter to begin a common noun. Capitalize a common noun only if it is the first word of a sentence. Some nouns are **proper nouns**. Capitalize a proper noun.

EXAMPLES	Common Nouns	Proper Nouns
	athlete	Carl Lewis
	city	Houston
	building	Shea Stadium
	day	Tuesday

2. An **adjective** usually begins with a lowercase letter. Capitalize an adjective only when it is a **proper adjective**. Proper adjectives are formed from proper nouns.

EXAMPLES	Proper Nouns	Proper Adjectives
	Islam	Islamic
	Africa	African

3. Capitalize parts of the country but not compass directions.

EXAMPLES	Ms. Lentz lives in the South.
	She lives south of our house.

4. Capitalize the names of languages. Capitalize the name of a course that has a number. Do not capitalize the names of school subjects except languages.

EXAMPLES	Sign up for Music 101.
	Who is taking music and history?

5. Capitalize the first, last, and all important words in a title.

EXAMPLE	I read *The Heart Is a Lonely Hunter.*

Activity A   Read the following sentences. List the bold words on your paper. Capitalize them only if they are proper nouns or proper adjectives.

1) **Derek** watched the **american** runners at the **olympics**. He decided to join the **track team** at **springfield high school**.

2) To prepare, he ran five **miles** every **day** except **friday**.

3) He tried out at a **cross-country course** at **macarthur park** last **weekend**.

4) He crossed the **finish line** in sixteen **minutes** and impressed **coach jones**.

5) "I think we can use you, young **man**," said the smiling **coach**. "The **springfield springers** may have a future **winner**."

Activity B   Read each set of sentences below. Decide which sentence uses correct capitalization. Write the letter of the correct sentence on your paper.

1) **a)** what is the name of your high school?
   b) What is the name of your High School?
   c) What is the name of your high school?

2) **a)** Order french toast for breakfast.
   b) Order French toast for breakfast.
   c) Order French Toast for breakfast.

3) **a)** When did the Blue Jays win the world series?
   b) When did the Blue Jays win the World Series?
   c) When did the blue jays win the World Series?

4) **a)** The bank is north of Bigelow avenue.
   b) The Bank is North of Bigelow Avenue.
   c) The bank is north of Bigelow Avenue.

5) **a)** The book *Narrative of the Life of Frederick Douglass* was written long ago.
   b) The book *Narrative Of The Life Of Frederick Douglass* was written long ago.
   c) The book *Narrative of the life of Frederick Douglass* was written long ago.

Check your writing for careful use of capital and lowercase letters. Review these rules.

- Always capitalize the first word in a sentence.
- Always capitalize the pronoun *I*.
- Capitalize proper nouns and proper adjectives.
- Capitalize parts of the country, languages, exact course names, and important words in a title.
- Do not capitalize common nouns.

Part A   Number your paper from 1 to 10. Read each of the following sentences. If the sentence is correct, write *Correct* after the number. If the sentence has a capitalization error, rewrite the sentence correctly after the number.

1) Thanksgiving is an American Holiday.
2) Mr. Chang teaches english at the High School.
3) My mother was born in North Carolina.
4) Did you receive any Valentines last february 14?
5) The last book Amanda read was *Kiss of Death*.
6) The football team in Springfield is called the Cubs.
7) what is the most popular Television Show this year?
8) Laura said, "i want to learn to play Chess."
9) Coronado was a spanish explorer who reached the southwest.
10) New York was once a Dutch colony.

Part B   Write one sentence about each of the following topics. Follow the rules for correct capitalization and punctuation.

1) A movie you have seen (include the title)
2) A place you have visited
3) Something that happened at your school (include the school name)
4) Someone in your family
5) Something that happens on a particular day of the week

Every sentence must have a verb. A verb is a word expressing action or state of being. Study the examples below.

1. A verb can express action in a sentence. **Action verbs** tell what the subject does or did.

> **EXAMPLES** Derek **runs** five miles almost every day.
>
> Amanda **met** Laura at the corner.

2. A verb can also express a condition of someone or something. A **state-of-being verb** does not suggest action.

> **EXAMPLES** Amanda and Laura **are** friends.
>
> Derek **seems** friendly, too.

3. A verb can be made of more than one word. A main verb often has a **helping verb**. The helping verb helps complete the meaning of the main verb. The helping verb plus the main verb form a **verb phrase**.

> **EXAMPLES** Derek **will jog** tomorrow.
>
> Cal and Denise **have been** friends for years.
>
> Everyone **should leave** at noon.

Activity A Write the verb or verb phrase in each of these sentences on your paper.

1) Every sentence has a verb.

2) You need a verb in every sentence.

3) Everyone must know the rules.

4) Soon you will be an expert!

5) Find the verb in this sentence.

Verb Phrases

A verb phrase includes a helping verb and a main verb. The main verb expresses action or state of being. The helping verb helps to express time. Study the following list of common helping verbs.

have	am	was	been	will	would	must
has	is	were	do	shall	could	may
had	are	be	did	can	should	might

A verb phrase has only one main verb. It may have more than one helping verb. The main verb is always last. Study the bold verb phrases in the sentences below. The helping verbs are underlined.

EXAMPLES   By nine in the morning, Derek <u>had</u> **trained** for an hour.

He <u>has</u> **been** **running** on the track every afternoon.

Activity B   Find the verb phrase in each sentence. Copy the verb phrase on your paper. Underline each helping verb.

1) Amanda was writing a letter to her aunt.

2) Cal has been playing in a band for a year.

3) The band is practicing now.

4) Laura must go to the gym this evening.

5) Amanda has known Laura for several years.

6) Mr. Chang has given the class a difficult assignment.

7) He will collect the papers tomorrow.

8) Coach Jones might make an announcement Friday.

9) The students did answer correctly.

10) You should have arrived sooner!

Tense

People talk and write about events that happen at different times. They use verbs to express **tense**. Study the following examples of six verb tenses:

EXAMPLES

Present:	Derek **starts** his training today.
Past:	Derek **started** his training yesterday.
Future:	Derek **will start** his training tomorrow.
Present perfect:	Derek **has started** his training.
Past perfect:	Derek **had started** his training earlier.
Future perfect:	Derek **will have started** his training by next Tuesday.

Activity C Read the paragraph below. Find the bold verbs or verb phrases. List each one on your paper. Label it with the verb tense.

HIGH SCHOOL STUDENT TRAINS FOR COUNTY MEET

Today Derek Corelli **announced** his training plan for the County Meet. When he **talked** with reporters, he already **had started** his training. Derek **runs** at least five miles every day. He said he **will have run** thirty miles by the end of this week. He always **takes** Friday off. He **will enter** some local meets soon. Corelli **has planned** for more training. Springfield High School **wishes** you luck, Derek!

Consistency of Tenses

Consistent
Following the same rules; staying the same.

As a writer, you must decide whether the tense of each verb is logical. All the verbs in a sentence should be **consistent**. Some sentences may include more than one main verb. Generally, all verbs should be in the same tense if the actions occur at the same time. However, different tenses can show that actions occur at different times. Study the following examples.

> **EXAMPLES**
>
> Since Derek **wanted** to win, he **practiced** every day.
> (Both verbs are past tense.)
>
> Every weekday Amanda **gets** up and **goes** to school.
> (Both verbs are present tense.)
>
> Mike **hopes** that Derek **will win** the race.
> (The verb *hopes* is present tense. The verb phrase *will win* is future tense. Right now, Mike hopes that Derek will win in the future.)

Activity D   Read each pair of sentences below. Study the bold verbs. Decide which sentence shows correct, consistent use of tenses. Write the letter of the correct sentence on your paper.

1) a) When Amanda **smiles**, the room **seems** brighter.

   b) When Amanda **smiled**, the room **seems** brighter.

2) a) The starting gun **fired**, and the runners **dashed** off!

   b) The starting gun **fired**, and the runners **dash** off!

3) a) As Derek **jogged** around the track, he **waved** to his friends.

   b) As Derek **jogs** around the track, he **waved** to his friends.

4) a) **Pay** attention to verbs, and your writing **improves**.

   b) **Pay** attention to verbs, and your writing **will improve**.

5) a) Because Derek **trained** hard, he **has raced** well.

   b) Because Derek **trained** hard, he **raced** well.

To write clear sentences, pay attention to verbs.

- Make sure that you have used the correct verb tense.
- Make sure that your verb tenses are consistent.

Part A Find the verbs in the following sentences. Check the tense. Correct any mistakes. Rewrite the verbs correctly.

The Big Race
by Derek Corelli

1) Last Saturday I look forward to my first big race.

2) That morning the alarm sounded, and I jump up.

3) My mother fixes me a good breakfast and I ate it all.

4) I had already ask Ms. Lentz about having the day off.

5) "I believe that you will succeed," my mother remarks to me.

6) My stomach churns and I tensed up, too.

7) I never doubted that I want to win that race.

8) When the race ended, I celebrate.

9) Now I plan for next week's race, which I intended to win, too!

10) I practice every day next week.

Part B Practice using verbs correctly. Write ten sentences about a topic of your choice. Here are suggested topics:

- A school event
- A book, a movie, or a television show
- A sport
- Use of technology

Number your sentences. Underline the verbs and verb phrases. (You may have more than one verb in a sentence.)

Most of the verbs in the English language are regular. To form the past tense of a regular verb, you add *-ed* or *-d*. You may also want to write the present perfect, past perfect, and future perfect tenses of a regular verb. To write the perfect tenses, you add *-ed* or *-d* to form the **past participle** of a regular verb. Below are two examples of regular verbs. Notice that the past tense and the past participle are the same.

Past participle

A principal part of a verb, used to form the perfect tenses.

EXAMPLES		
Regular verb:		*to paint*
Present tense:		the man *paints*, they *paint*
Past tense:		he *painted*
Past participle used to form perfect tense:		she has *painted*
Regular verb:		*to promise*
Present tense:		I *promise*, she *promises*
Past tense:		they *promised*
Past participle used to form perfect tense:		they have *promised*

Activity A   Write six sentences that include the regular verb *stop*. Write one sentence for each of the tenses listed below. (Look at the examples above for models.)

Present

Past

Future

Present perfect

Past perfect

Future perfect

Now write a sentence that includes the regular verb *dance* in each of the tenses listed.

	Irregular verb

Irregular verb

A verb that does not form its past and past participle by adding -ed to the present tense form. (eat, ate, eaten)

Some verbs are not regular. **Irregular verbs** change their forms in the different tenses. Two common irregular verbs are *be* and *have*. Study their forms.

Verb	Present	Past	Past Participle
be	am, is, are	was, were	been
have	has, have	had	had

Activity B   Write a sentence to answer each question below. Use a form of the verb *be* or *have* in each of your answers. Underline the verb in your sentence.

1) Where were you this morning?

2) Where are you now?

3) What have you had to eat today?

4) How long have you been here?

5) What is your favorite sport?

6) Which team has good players?

Study the irregular verbs in the table below.

Present	Past	Past Participle
begin	began	begun
bend	bent	bent
bite	bit	bitten
blow	blew	blown
break	broke	broken
bring	brought	brought
burst	burst	burst
buy	bought	bought

Activity C Write the correct form of the verb for each of the following sentences. Remember that the past participle is used with *has, have,* or *had.*

1) The bottle in the freezer has (burst).

2) The wind (blow) the old tree over yesterday.

3) We have finally (begin) the lesson.

4) Last week we (buy) new tires.

5) That gate (break) years ago.

6) He (bend) over and touched his toes.

7) He (bite) into a juicy apple.

8) They (bring) a chocolate cake to the party.

9) The teacher (begin) to speak.

10) What has the dog (break)?

Activity D Write each word below in a correct sentence. Use the word as a verb.

1) burst

2) bought

3) blew

4) bent

5) begun

6) bitten

7) began

8) blown

9) broken

10) bit

Study the irregular verbs in the table below.

Present	Past	Past Participle
catch	caught	caught
choose	chose	chosen
come	came	come
cost	cost	cost
cut	cut	cut
dig	dug	dug
do	did	done
draw	drew	drawn
drink	drank	drunk
drive	drove	driven

Activity E   Change each bold verb to either the past tense or to the past participle form. Write the correct sentence on your paper.

1) Last night Laura **do** her homework.

2) The coach has **choose** the starting players.

3) We have already **dig** our garden.

4) Yesterday I **drive** my old car to work.

5) She had **drink** a glass of water before lunch.

6) You have **draw** a clear picture.

Activity F   Find the verb that is not correct. Rewrite the verb correctly.

1) "You done a fine job on this report," Mike said.

2) Last year that coat costed only sixty-five dollars.

3) "I cutted my finger!" the worker cried.

4) Almost all of my friends come to our last party.

5) I have finally did all of my work.

6) They caughted eight large fish.

Study the irregular verbs in the table below.

Present	Past	Past Participle
eat	ate	eaten
fall	fell	fallen
feed	fed	fed
feel	felt	felt
fight	fought	fought
find	found	found
fly	flew	flown
forget	forgot	forgotten
forgive	forgave	forgiven
freeze	froze	frozen

Activity G   Change each bold verb to either the past tense or the past participle form. Rewrite the sentences correctly.

1) Last year Mr. Corelli **flied** to Canada on business.

2) "I nearly **freezed** to death up there," he said.

3) He saw a woman who had **fell** on the ice.

4) "I **fighted** to stay on my feet myself," he said.

5) "I have **forgave** my boss for sending me on this trip," he said.

6) Mr. Corelli **finded** a wonderful gift for his wife.

7) He **eaten** in the hotel restaurant every night.

8) "They **feeded** me very well," he told his family.

9) After he **flown** home, he gave his wife the present.

10) "I have not **forget** you," he told his wife.

11) Ms. Corelli opened the box and **felted** the soft wool throw.

12) "You **founded** the perfect gift," she told her husband.

13) Mr. Corelli **feeled** that the trip was interesting.

Study the irregular verbs in the table below.

Present	Past	Past Participle
get	got	got, gotten
give	gave	given
go	went	gone
grow	grew	grown
hear	heard	heard
hide	hid	hidden
hit	hit	hit
keep	kept	kept
know	knew	known

Activity H Change each bold verb to either the past tense or the past participle form. Rewrite the sentences correctly.

1) "Has Derek **went** yet?" asked Mike.

2) Aunt Marie has **gave** me a birthday gift.

3) Have you **hear** the latest news?

4) A storm **hitted** town last night.

5) Mr. Corelli, Derek's father, has **grew** a beard.

6) Mike **keeped** a flashlight in the car.

7) "I **knows** that I would win the race," said Derek.

8) Derek **get** down at the starting block and waited.

9) He waited until he **heared** the whistle.

10) Benjy **hided** his bone in the garden.

Study the irregular verbs in the table below.

Present	Past	Past Participle
lead	led	led
leave	left	left
lie	lay	lain
lose	lost	lost
make	made	made
mean	meant	meant
put	put	put
read	read	read
ride	rode	ridden
ring	rang	rung

Activity I Find the verb error in each sentence below. Write each sentence correctly.

1) That cowboy has never <u>rode</u> in a rodeo before.

2) She putted the groceries on the shelves.

3) The cat <u>lain</u> on the sofa all morning.

4) We all leaved work at five o'clock yesterday.

5) Who has rang the doorbell?

6) I have readed that book before.

Activity J Some verbs do not change their forms at all. Copy the verbs in these sentences. Decide whether each verb is present or past tense. Write *Present* or *Past* for each verb.

1) I **read** that book yesterday.

2) They **cut** fresh flowers every day.

3) Cooks often **put** on aprons.

4) Last week Jason **hit** a home run for the team.

5) Today apples **cost** less than yesterday.

Study the irregular verbs in the table below.

Present	Past	Past Participle
see	saw	seen
send	sent	sent
set	set	set
shake	shook	shaken
sing	sang	sung
sit	sat	sat
spread	spread	spread
stand	stood	stood
steal	stole	stolen
swear	swore	sworn
swim	swam	swum
swing	swung	swung

Activity K   Read the following sentences. Decide whether the past or the past participle form should be used. Write the correct verb forms.

1) The witness (swear) she heard the thief.

2) The man on trial had (steal) a ring.

3) Where have you (sing) before?

4) The batter (swing) but missed.

5) Paul (set) the vase on the table.

6) Someone has (sit) on this chair.

7) I have (stand) in line for hours!

8) Last summer we (swim) at the lake.

9) Have you (send) that package yet?

10) We (shake) the package, and it rattled.

11) We (spread) the tablecloth for the picnic.

12) Have you (see) Mike?

13) Yes, I (see) him in English class.

Study the irregular verbs in the table below.

Present	Past	Past Participle
take	took	taken
teach	taught	taught
tear	tore	torn
think	thought	thought
wake	woke	woken
wear	wore	worn
weep	wept	wept
win	won	won
wring	wrung	wrung
write	wrote	written

Activity L   Find the verb error in each of the following sentences. Rewrite the sentence using the correct verb form on your paper. Use the table above to help you.

1) At least once a year, Amanda has <u>wrote</u> to her aunt Frances.

2) The nurse <u>wringed</u> out the wet towel.

3) Everyone was glad that Derek <u>winned</u> the race.

4) Laura is glad that she has <u>took</u> Spanish 1.

5) Mike <u>thinked</u>, and then he answered the question.

6) Derek <u>weared</u> his good shoes to school.

7) "Thanks for this wonderful award," <u>weeped</u> the actor.

8) Who has <u>teared</u> a hole in this paper?

9) The fire alarm <u>wokened</u> everyone.

10) "Now that you have <u>teached</u> me all of these verbs, I will never make a mistake," said the student.

Remember to use and spell regular and irregular verb forms correctly.

Part A Write each verb below in a correct sentence. Write a different sentence for each word.

1) brought
2) fallen
3) taken
4) stood
5) driven
6) set
7) bit
8) came
9) caught
10) forgotten

Part B The bold verb in each sentence below is incorrect. Correct the sentence by changing the verb. You will need to change it either to the past or the past participle form. Write the verb on your paper.

1) Last night the ice **freeze** on the lake.
2) What have you **did**?
3) "I **swang** from that tree as a child," said Mr. Luca.
4) A robber has **stealed** the money.
5) "I **seen** him do it!" said the witness.
6) You have already **goed** to the gym once.
7) The tomato plants have **growed** tall.
8) The team **losed** the game by one point.
9) Amanda felt ill and **lied** in bed all morning.
10) The butterflies **fly** north last spring.

Possessive noun

A noun that names the owner of something or names a relationship between people or things. A possessive noun must have an apostrophe (Mary's coat; the woman's car; the voters' opinions).

Apostrophe

A punctuation mark used to replace missing letters in a contraction (doesn't) or to show possession (Mary's coat).

A **possessive noun** shows ownership or a relationship. You may confuse possessive nouns with plural nouns because the two forms sound alike: *dog's* and *dogs*, for example. Remember to use an **apostrophe** in a possessive noun—and NOT to use one in a plural noun.

Study the examples below. Notice the different spellings of the bold plural and possessive forms.

EXAMPLES	**Plurals**	**Possessives**
	The **friends** meet here.	The **friend's** house is nearby.
	The family has two **dogs**.	The spotted **dog's** collar is broken.
	Two **cars** are parked on the street.	Which **car's** tire is flat?

Activity A   Read each sentence. Copy the bold plural nouns on your paper under the heading *Plurals*. The bold possessive nouns are missing apostrophes. Rewrite them correctly under the heading *Possessives*.

1) Both **teams** met at the stadium.

2) Where is the **poodles** leash?

3) Everyone in **Lauras** class liked learning Spanish.

4) Knowing about irregular **verbs** is important.

5) Where is **Benjys** collar?

6) Where are my running **shoes**?

Study these rules for forming singular and plural possessive nouns. Remember that the placement of an apostrophe makes your meaning clear.

1. If the noun is singular, add an apostrophe before the letter *s*.

EXAMPLES	Cal's house
	one child's room
	Jo Jones's car

2. If the noun is plural, add an apostrophe after the letter *s*.

EXAMPLES	states' rights
	two actors' parts
	cities' problems

Irregular plural noun

A noun that forms its plural in an unusual way, not with the usual -s or -es (mouse, mice; foot, feet; man, men).

3. Be careful with **irregular plural nouns**. If the plural does NOT end in *-s*, add an apostrophe before the letter *s*.

EXAMPLES	people's opinions
	children's game
	women's clothes

Activity B   Read each sentence. Decide whether the bold word is a singular possessive or a plural possessive. Write *Singular* or *Plural* after each number.

1) The **sisters'** room is painted blue.

2) What time is the **teachers'** meeting?

3) The students answered the **teacher's** questions.

4) **Men's** shirts are on sale.

5) The **dancer's** feet hurt.

Activity C Read the singular and plural forms of each of the words below. Write the singular possessive form and the plural possessive form of each word. Here are examples with the singular word *wolf* and the plural word *wolves*.

Examples Singular possessive: *wolf's* Plural possessive: *wolves'*

Singular	Plural
1) child	children
2) man	men
3) tree	trees
4) Wilson	Wilsons
5) family	families
6) boss	bosses
7) friend	friends
8) class	classes
9) team	teams
10) woman	women
11) baby	babies
12) shelf	shelves
13) goose	geese
14) mouse	mice
15) city	cities
16) animal	animals
17) artist	artists
18) day	days
19) uncle	uncles
20) Ruiz	Ruizes

Activity D   The letter below contains six errors in the use of possessives and plurals. List the incorrect words. Write the correct form for each.

May 4, 20--

Dear Ms. Quigley,

Laura and I enjoyed watching the rodeo with you in Centerville a few weeks' ago. We both liked the bucking broncs' very much. The riders skill was unbelievable. The rodeo clown's were also fun to watch. All of our friend's have heard about the rodeo. One of our best memories' is meeting you! We are looking forward to seeing you again.

Sincerely,
Amanda O'Hara

Pay attention to plural nouns and possessive nouns. Remember the rules for using them correctly.

- Do NOT add an apostrophe to make a plural noun. Most of the time, just add -*s*.
- Add apostrophe -*s* to make a singular possessive noun.
- Add just an apostrophe to make a plural possessive noun.
- If the plural noun is irregular, add apostrophe -*s* to make it a possessive.

Part A Choose the correct sentence in each pair below. Write the letter of that sentence on your paper.

1) a) The Wilsons' home is on Third Street.
b) The Wilson's home is on Third Street.

2) a) Both team's were ready for the big event.
b) Both teams were ready for the big event.

3) a) Childrens' toys were scattered everywhere.
b) Children's toys were scattered everywhere.

4) a) My neighbors cat climbed up a tree.
b) My neighbor's cat climbed up a tree.

5) a) The fire department brought some ladders.
b) The fire department brought some ladder's.

Part B Write the possessive form of each word below. Use the possessive form in a sentence.

1) neighbors

2) baby

3) people

4) teacher

5) mice

Chapter 3 Review

Part A   Choose the word that correctly completes each sentence. Write the word on your paper.

1) The leaves on the tree (is, are) red.

2) The movie *Take the (money, Money) and Run* is silly.

3) What is the tallest (building, Building) in the world?

4) Denise went with Cal and (I, me) to the game.

5) Yankee (stadium, Stadium) is in New York.

6) The library has a (childrens', children's) room.

7) Today Derek has (ran, run) five miles.

8) The campers (catched, caught) fish for dinner.

9) The referee (saw, seen) the foul.

10) How many (families', families) live in this house?

Part B   Find the one error in each sentence below. Then write each sentence correctly on your paper.

1) Each of the students are ready to begin.

2) "My favorite class is english," said Denise.

3) The novelist Jack London wrote *The Call Of the Wild*.

4) All of the students remembered them books.

5) Every pronoun must agree with their antecedent.

6) Rain and snow often falls in November.

7) Denise gave her friend her lunch.

8) They say that children watch too much TV.

9) Derek knew that he want to win that race.

10) When the race were over, Derek jogged happily around the track.

Part C Read each set of sentences. Decide which one is correct. Write the letter of that sentence on your paper.

1) a) We have driven fifty miles.
   b) We have drived fifty miles.
   c) We have driven fifty mile's.

2) a) The twin's do not look at all alike.
   b) The twins do not look at all alike.
   c) The twins' do not look at all alike.

3) a) The runners has broke a record!
   b) The runners have broke a record!
   c) The runners have broken a record!

4) a) The Hongs live west of Southville.
   b) The Hongs' live west of Southville.
   c) The Hongs live West of Southville.

5) a) Who wrote the book *Nothing But the Truth?*
   b) Who wrote the book *Nothing but the truth?*
   c) Who has wrote the book *Nothing but the Truth?*

Part D Follow each direction.

1) Write a sentence in which a pronoun is used as the subject.

2) Write a sentence that includes a possessive pronoun.

3) Write a sentence in which at least one of the verbs is in the future tense.

4) Write a sentence containing a singular possessive noun.

5) Write a sentence containing a plural possessive noun.

Test Taking Tip When taking a short-answer test, first answer the questions you know. Then go back to spend time on the questions you are less sure of.

Spelling Counts!

4

Most of the writing you will do in your lifetime will be for others to read. Be kind to your readers! Don't confuse them by writing one word when you mean another. Don't let misspelled words slow down your readers. Don't let misspellings make your readers think your message is not important. Your message *is* important. Make sure each word says what you mean.

Memorize the spelling of the words you use often. Keep a dictionary handy to check the spelling of words you use less often.

In Chapter 4, you will learn spelling rules and patterns. You will practice spelling words correctly.

Goals for Learning

▶ To choose the right homonym or the right word from easily confused pairs

▶ To use apostrophes correctly

▶ To spell plural nouns correctly

▶ To spell words with endings correctly

▶ To memorize the spellings of words that are often misspelled

Homonyms

Words that sound alike but have different meanings and spellings.

Say these words aloud: *to, two, too*. These words are **homonyms**. The English language has many sound-alike words, or homonyms. Make sure that you spell the homonym that fits with your meaning. Study the meanings and examples below.

to	Moving toward or showing a relationship. The bus drove **to** Dallas. Let's walk **to** the store. Stand next **to** me!	**too**	Very; also. I ate **too** much. Did you eat a lot, **too**?
to	A word used before a verb. We like **to** dance, **to** sing, and **to** have a good time.	**two**	A number. It is **two** o'clock. Do you want one or **two** bananas?

Activity A   Read each sentence below. Write the homonyms that correctly complete each sentence.

1) Mike ran (to, too, two) miles (to, too, two) get (to, too, two) school in time.

2) Mike was (to, too, two) out of breath (to, too, two) talk.

3) We have (to, too, two) questions (to, too, two) ask the mayor.

4) "I, (to, too, two), would like (to, too, two) know the answers," said the mayor.

5) If you have (to, too, two) many things (to, too, two) do at the same time, just do one or (to, too, two).

Activity B   Write one sentence on your paper that uses the words *to, too,* and *two*.

Activity C Read about each pair of homonyms. Rewrite each sentence using the correct homonym.

| all ready | Completely prepared. We are **all ready** for the party. | already | Before; previously. We have **already** finished our work. |

1) Derek is (all ready, already) for his next race.

2) Derek has (all ready, already) won his first race.

3) The students have done their homework (all ready, already).

4) Are we (all ready, already) for the show?

| hear | To receive a sound through the ears. I **hear** you loud and clear. | here | In this place. We'll meet **here** later. |

5) Did you (hear, here) the news?

6) I did not (hear, here) what you said.

7) Laura will be (hear, here) soon.

8) Which people were (hear, here) first?

| weak | Not strong. Illness makes people feel **weak**. | week | Seven days. Carlos works two evenings a **week**. |

9) Ms. Lentz likes to drink (weak, week) tea.

10) Derek runs thirty miles every (weak, week).

11) This is the third (weak, week) of the month.

12) Have you ever felt (weak, week) in the knees?

Activity D Read about each pair of homonyms. Write the homonym that correctly completes each sentence.

piece	A part or section. Take another **piece** of pie.	**peace**	The absence of war; calm. Can we have some **peace** and quiet, please?

1) One (piece, peace) is missing from the puzzle.

2) The town set aside a (piece, peace) of land for a park.

3) The fighting stopped, and (piece, peace) arrived at last.

4) Put a (piece, peace) of cheese on that sandwich.

whether	A word used to introduce two choices. **Whether** the team wins or loses, it will still be in the playoffs.	**weather**	The condition of the atmosphere at a certain time and place. The **weather** changed from hot to cold.

5) The (whether, weather) is clear and sunny today.

6) Derek does not know (whether, weather) to go to his job.

7) Can you tell (whether, weather) it will rain?

8) It is not easy to forecast the (whether, weather) in New England.

waist	Part of the body between hips and ribs. A belt fits around the **waist**.	**waste**	Trash; to use up carelessly. That basket is for **waste**. Do not **waste** paper.

9) Those pants are too big around the (waist, waste).

10) The factory dumped (waist, waste) into the river.

11) Do not (waist, waste) your time.

12) Step into the water up to your (waist, waste).

Activity E Read about each pair of homonyms. Rewrite each sentence using the correct homonym.

brake	Something that stops or slows motion; to stop or slow the motion. The driver used the **brake** to **brake** the car.	**break**	To separate into pieces; an interruption or pause. Did that cup **break** while you were on a coffee **break**?

1) The TV show had one commercial (brake, break).

2) The child did not mean to (brake, break) the window.

3) When you wish to (brake, break), step on the pedal.

4) Mike needs to fix the (brake, break) on his bicycle.

past	Of a time gone by; times that have gone by. We studied the **past** and learned about **past** events.	**passed**	Past tense of pass. The student **passed** the test.

5) During the (past, passed) week, Derek ran thirty miles.

6) When he ran, Derek (past, passed) Ms. Lentz's station.

7) Derek was happy when he (past, passed) his test.

8) The storm finally (past, passed).

council	A group that meets to discuss issues or to govern. The town **council** has six members.	**counsel**	Advice; to give advice. The king ignored his minister's wise **counsel**. The minister tried to **counsel** against war.

9) The teacher offered to (council, counsel) the student.

10) The student listened to the teacher's (council, counsel).

11) The student (council, counsel) meets every week.

12) The (council, counsel) voted against a tax increase.

Activity F Read about each pair or set of homonyms. Write the homonym that correctly completes each sentence.

through	Finished; in and out of. We will be **through** with our trip after we pass **through** this tunnel.	**threw**	Past tense of throw. Who **threw** that tomato?

1) Mike walked (through, threw) the door.
2) Mike (through, threw) the basketball to Derek.
3) We hope that your troubles are (through, threw).
4) The storm passed (through, threw) quickly.

plain	Clear and simple; not fancy. The woman wore a **plain** dress.	**plane**	A woodworking tool for making a surface smooth and flat; to use a plane to smooth a surface. The carpenter used a **plane** to **plane** the shelf.
plain	A flat area of land. Grass grew on the **plain**.		
plane	A flat surface; an airplane. The math students learned about lines that form a **plane**.		

5) "I like (plain, plane) cooking," said Mr. O'Hara.
6) Have you ever flown on a (plain, plane)?
7) Settlers found good farmland on the (plain, plane).
8) Before you sand the wood, (plain, plane) it.

their	Belonging to them. All the students have **their** homework.	**there**	A word used to introduce a sentence. **There** are three children in the family.
there	At that place or time. Park the car over **there**.	**they're**	A shortened form of *they are*. If Luis and Tom are late, **they're** in trouble.

9) (Their, There, They're) is more than one way to solve a problem.
10) Which towns have (their, there, they're) own libraries?
11) We're driving to Savannah. Will it take us long to get (their, there, they're)?

Activity G Read about each set of homonyms. Rewrite each sentence using the correct homonym.

principal	First in importance; the head of a school. What is the **principal** job of a school **principal**?	**principle**	A basic truth; a rule. The **principle** of freedom must be protected.
principal	The amount of money on which interest is charged or paid. Loan payments include interest and **principal**.		

1) The _____ city of Massachusetts is Boston.

2) We hope our leaders have high _____.

3) This bank charges high interest on the _____ of a loan.

4) An important _____ in America is freedom.

5) The _____ of the middle school is Mr. Chang.

capital	The city in which state or national government is based; relating to the seat of government. Washington, D.C. is the **capital** of the United States. What is the **capital** city of your state?	**capital**	A sum of money. To set up a business, a person needs **capital**.
		capitol	A building in which state lawmakers meet. The state **capitol** has a statue on top of it.
capital	An uppercase letter. A proper noun begins with a **capital**.	**Capitol**	The building in Washington, D.C. in which the Congress of the United States meets. The senator spoke on the steps of the **Capitol**.
capital	Punishable by death. Treason is a **capital** crime.		

6) Mr. Takemura visited Paris, the _____ of France.

7) Always use a _____ letter to begin the name of a month.

8) Mike visited the _____ in Washington, D.C.

9) The two women agreed to combine their _____ to start a business.

10) A golden dome is on the _____ in Des Moines, Iowa.

11) Would it be unjust to make burglary a _____ offense?

Homonyms are words that sound alike but have different meanings and spellings. When you are writing, you must think about which meaning you want your readers to understand. Then use the spelling that matches that meaning.

Part A   Choose the word in parentheses that correctly completes the sentence. Write the word on your paper.

1) The members of the queen's (counsel, council) met in a large hall.

2) Is the (whether, weather) expected to turn cloudy?

3) What city is the (capitol, capital, Capitol) of Ecuador?

4) No one could (here, hear) the speaker.

5) Adults may make (there, their, they're) own decisions.

6) After being rescued, the woman said, "My life (past, passed) before my eyes!"

7) "To be honest with others has been my (principle, principal) rule in life," said Mr. Corelli.

8) "Say, Dad," Derek said. "I seem to need a little (capital, capitol, Capitol)."

9) "I'll make you a loan. You can repay the (principal, principle) at five dollars a week."

10) "OK, that's not (to, too, two) much," Derek agreed.

Part B   Write an original sentence with each word below.

1) through

2) threw

3) waste

4) waist

5) weak

6) week

7) plain

8) plane

9) already

10) break

Some pairs of English words can confuse a speller. The words look and sound *almost* alike. It helps to pronounce each word exactly. Then you can choose the correct spelling.

Be sure to choose the spelling that fits your meaning. Try using the word in your sentence. Look at the dictionary to be sure you have the spelling that fits your meaning.

Compare the spellings of these two words. Pronounce each one carefully. Read about their different meanings and uses.

advice	Suggestions or information. Used as a noun. The counselor gave helpful **advice**.	**advise**	To give suggestions or information. Used as a verb. What did the counselor **advise** you to do?

Activity A   Read each sentence below. Write the word on your paper that correctly completes each sentence.

1) The president's cabinet gives him (advice, advise).

2) Cabinet members (advice, advise) the president.

3) Some people like to give (advice, advise) to others.

4) People don't always take others' (advice, advise).

5) "I need someone to (advice, advise) me," said Mike.

6) The counselor gave Mike useful (advice, advise).

Activity B Read about each pair of words. Write the word on your paper that correctly completes each sentence.

than	A word used in a comparison. Jon's feet are bigger **than** his father's.	**then**	At that time; soon afterward. **Then** what happened?

1) Laura likes swimming more (than, then) tennis.

2) Back (than, then), my family lived in Mexico.

3) I think that Amanda is older (than, then) Laura.

4) First we cried, and (than, then) we laughed.

quite	Completely; truly. I am not **quite** done reading.	**quiet**	Silent; making almost no noise. It's peaceful and **quiet** here.

5) We took a walk through the (quite, quiet) woods.

6) We took (quite, quiet) a long walk!

7) This car has such a (quite, quiet) ride!

8) "Please be (quite, quiet)," said the librarian.

were	Past tense of the verb *be*. The children **were** in bed.	**where**	At or in what place. **Where** did the children sleep?

9) (Were, Where) is Mexico?

10) We (were, where) waiting for you for an hour!

11) Carlos and his brother (were, where) sharing a room.

12) "I do not know (were, where) I put my glasses," said Mr. Corelli.

Activity C   Read about each pair of words. Rewrite each
sentence using the word that correctly completes it.

affect	To influence someone or something. Used as a verb. How does hot weather **affect** you?	effect	The result; the influence that one thing has on something else. Used as a noun. One **effect** of cold weather is dry skin.

1) Sleepiness is one side (affect, effect) of this medicine.

2) The sad song had no (affect, effect) on Valerie.

3) Smoke from factories does (affect, effect) air quality.

personal	Private; having to do with a particular person. A diary is a **personal** form of writing.	personnel	The employees of a business. A company vice president was in charge of **personnel**.

4) Send your job application to the (personal, personnel) office.

5) Please lock your (personal, personnel) belongings in the safe.

6) This is a (personal, personnel) matter between my friend and me.

formally	In a formal or socially polite way; according to ceremony or rules. The guests dressed **formally** for the wedding.	formerly	Of a former, or earlier, time. Computers now do much of the work **formerly** done by bank tellers.

7) The city held a parade to honor the hero (formally, formerly).

8) Ms. Hall (formally, formerly) lived in Chicago.

9) Do you know how to write (formally, formerly)?

Activity D   Read about each pair of words. Write the word on your paper that correctly completes each sentence.

loose	Free; not tight. Used as an adjective. **Loose** clothing is in style.	**lose**	To misplace; to fail to win. Used as a verb. One team must **lose**.

1) Laura preferred a (loose, lose) belt.

2) Did you (loose, lose) your money?

3) I hope that Derek does not (loose, lose) the race.

4) Don't let Benjy get (loose, lose); he might run away.

choose	To pick out or select. In a democracy, voters **choose** their leaders.	**chose**	Past tense of *to choose;* picked out or selected. (The word *chose* is never used with a helping verb such as *must, did, have,* or *should.*) Last month the voters **chose** their leaders.

5) "Did you (choose, chose) your dessert yet?" asked Laura.

6) "Yes, I (choose, chose) the orange," said Amanda.

7) "I think I will (choose, chose) the pineapple," said Laura.

8) "Maybe I should (choose, chose) the banana," said Amanda.

accept	To receive willingly. Used as a verb. I **accept** your apology.	**except**	Other than; if not for the fact that; but. Everyone was there **except** me.

9) Laura always says, "I have everything I need (accept, except) money."

10) Amanda would not (accept, except) the gift.

11) The company did (accept, except) Mike for the job.

12) That cat never comes home (accept, except) to eat.

Words that sound nearly alike can confuse spellers. When you write, choose the spelling that fits with your meaning. Pronounce the word especially carefully to remember which spelling fits.

Part A Read the sentence or sentences. Choose the word in parentheses that correctly completes each sentence. Write the words in the correct order on your paper.

1) Amanda always thought she was more interested in art (then, than) math, but (then, than) she discovered geometry.

2) "I can give you (advise, advice)," said Ms. Lawson. "But I also (advise, advice) you to make your own decision."

3) Students (formerly, formally) dressed more (formerly, formally) for school than they do today.

4) At day's end, Mr. Corelli felt (quiet, quite) tired. He hoped for a (quiet, quite) evening at home.

5) How did the storm (affect, effect) the land? The loss of trees was one (affect, effect).

6) Someone in the (personal, personnel) department may be able to help workers who have (personal, personnel) problems.

7) Laura feared she might (lose, loose) the ring because it was so (lose, loose) on her finger.

8) Ms. O'Hara wondered (were, where) the lost keys (were, where).

9) Mike (choose, chose) a course that would help him (choose, chose) a career.

10) "I will (accept, except) every excuse (accept, except) laziness," said Mr. Chang.

Part B Write one original sentence for each word below.

1) personal   4) formerly
2) quiet   5) chose
3) except

Contraction

A shortened form of one or two words. An apostrophe stands for the missing letters (they're, he'll, jumpin').

In Chapter 3, you saw how an apostrophe (') is used to show possession in nouns. Notice the apostrophe in these three examples: *Marie's dog, the students' homework, the children's room.*

The apostrophe is also used to stand for missing letters in a **contraction.**

Contractions are most often used in informal writing—notes and friendly letters, for example. You may want to use contractions to show spoken words in dialogue, too.

Here is a list of some commonly used contractions. They are all made of a verb and the word *not.*

aren't = are not		**hasn't** = has not	
isn't = is not		**haven't** = have not	
can't = cannot		**hadn't** = had not	
doesn't = does not		**wouldn't** = would not	
don't = do not		**couldn't** = could not	
weren't = were not		**shouldn't** = should not	
won't = will not		**didn't** = did not	

Activity A   Find the eight contractions in the following paragraphs. Rewrite each contraction correctly on your paper.

> Derek Corelli hadnt missed a day of practice in weeks. He wouldnt go anywhere but the track.
> "Shouldnt your coach give you a rest?" asked his mother. "Arent you working too hard?"
> "I want to be ready for the next meet," Derek replied. "I havent got much time left."
> "I sent a note to Aunt Lydia," said Ms. Corelli. "She doesnt want to miss your event. We will cheer for you. But please dont worry about winning or losing. Just have fun!"
> "That is what mothers are supposed to say," said Derek. "But losing isnt in my plans!"

Here are more contractions. Study the list.

I'd = I would, I had	**we'll** = we will
I'll = I will	**we're** = we are
I'm = I am	**we've** = we have
I've = I have	**they'd** = they would, they had
you'll = you will	**they're** = they are
you're = you are	**they've** = they have
you've = you have	**that's** = that is, that has
he's = he is, he has	**what's** = what is, what has
she's = she is, she has	**who's** = who is, who has
it's = it is, it has	**there's** = there is
let's = let us	**here's** = here is

Activity B Rewrite the bold words as contractions on your paper.

1) **I had** never seen a rodeo before.

2) Now **I would** like to see a rodeo again.

3) Amanda says that **she has** never been in a plane.

4) The Leungs say that **they are** sure that **they will** take the trip.

5) **It is** true that **they have** gone.

6) **There is** still time to get to a movie, so **let us** find out **what is** playing.

Some possessive pronouns and contractions are homonyms. They sound alike. Only the contraction is spelled with an apostrophe, however. Be careful NOT to use an apostrophe with a possessive pronoun. Two commonly confused homonyms are *its* and *it's*.

its	A possessive pronoun used to show ownership. Do you see that house? **Its** roof needs fixing.	**it's**	A contraction of *it is*. Whenever **it's** raining, the roof leaks.

Activity C Read the sentences. Choose the word or words that correctly complete the sentence. Write the words in the correct order on your paper.

1) "That kitten is crying. I think (its, it's) hungry," said Laura.

2) "I wonder where (its, it's) owner is," she added.

3) "(Its, It's) name is on (its, it's) collar," said Amanda.

4) She looked at (its, it's) tag. "(Its, It's) called Fluffy."

5) "(Its, It's) friendly," said Amanda as the kitten purred and licked (its, it's) fur.

6) Then Fluffy trotted off to (its, it's) home.

Study the definitions and example sentences for the following homonyms. Notice that the possessive pronouns do NOT have apostrophes.

your	A possessive pronoun used to show ownership.	**whose**	A possessive pronoun used to show ownership.
you're	A contraction of *you are*. If **you're** late for practice, **your** coach may be angry.	**who's**	A contraction of *who is* or *who has*. Who's that tall player? No one knows **whose** team he is on.

Activity D Look for the words *your, you're, whose,* and *who's* in the sentences below. Copy each correct word on your paper. Rewrite each incorrect word.

1) "Where are your shoes, Derek?" asked the coach.

2) "I don't know," Derek said. "Whose seen my lucky shoes?"

3) "Do you all have you're own shoes?" the coach asked the team.

4) "Aren't you're shoes always in your bag?" asked the coach.

5) "Look whose coming! Look whose shoes Benjy has!"

6) "Your a good dog, Benjy," cried Derek.

Study the definitions and example sentences for the following homonyms. Notice that the possessive pronouns do NOT have apostrophes.

their	A possessive pronoun used to show ownership.	**theirs**	A possessive pronoun used to show ownership.
they're	A contraction of *they are*.	**there's**	A contraction of *there is*.
	Springfield fans wait for **their** team to score. **They're** ready to give a big cheer.		**There's** a mixup over sandwiches. Which sandwiches are ours? Which are yours? Which are **theirs**?

Activity E Choose the word that correctly completes the sentence. Write the word on your paper.

1) "(Theirs, There's) my dad!" Derek called out.

2) Derek's parents waved from (their, they're) seats in the stands.

3) When your neighbors are home, please ring (their, they're) bell.

4) If (there's, theirs) no answer, leave a note.

5) We made our plans, and they made (there's, theirs).

6) (There's, Theirs) no chance to change our plans.

To spell a word that may or may not have an apostrophe, remember these rules.

- A contraction must have an apostrophe. The apostrophe stands for the missing letters.
- A possessive pronoun NEVER has an apostrophe.
- When a possessive pronoun and a contraction are homonyms, be especially careful. Remember to use the spelling that fits with your meaning.

Part A Read Derek's paragraphs. Find ten mistakes made with contractions. Write each word correctly on your paper.

My Second Race

Im sure youve guessed by now that Ive won my second race. Id arrived at the track before eight in the morning. I just couldnt sleep! The competition wasnt so good at the first race. I must say, the second school wasnt much better! Ha!

"Ill win by several seconds," I said to myself.

And I did! Im planning to set a new record in my third race! Theres more to come, fans.

Part B Find the error in each of these sentences. Rewrite the sentence correctly on your paper.

1) Its about time they changed their minds!
2) If theres a problem, let's solve it.
3) Last month Derek was strong, but now hes' even stronger.
4) We'd like to join you're team.
5) "Your story isnt easy to believe," said the coach.
6) "There's a dog named Benjy thats fond of chewing up shoelaces," explained Derek.
7) Shouldn't you be resting before you're big game?
8) "If this isn't my coat, who's is it?" asked Mr. Corelli.
9) The dog needs it's walk; here's its leash.
10) Some of his friends are also her's.

A singular noun names one person, place, thing, or idea. A plural noun names more than one person, place, thing, or idea. Here are two rules for making plural nouns.

1. Add -*s* to make most nouns plural.

EXAMPLES	Singular	Plural
	noun	nouns
	rule	rules
	subject	subjects
	key	keys

2. If a noun ends in -*s*, -*z*, -*x*, -*sh*, or -*ch*, then add -*es* to make it plural.

EXAMPLES	Singular	Plural
	guess	guesses
	buzz	buzzes
	ax	axes
	leash	leashes
	watch	watches

Activity A Write the plural form of each of these singular nouns on your paper.

1) speech

2) teacher

3) house

4) waltz

5) branch

6) dish

7) beach

8) shoe

9) school

10) race

11) box

12) word

13) noun

14) letter

15) church

16) fox

17) desk

18) paper

19) bus

20) book

Nouns Ending With -y

Some nouns end with a vowel before the letter *y*. If there is a vowel before *y*, just add -*s* to make a plural noun. (The vowels include *a, e, i, o,* and *u.*)

EXAMPLES	Singular	Plural
	boy	boys
	monkey	monkeys
	guy	guys
	relay	relays

Some nouns end with a consonant before the *y*. Then you must change the *y* to *i* and add -*es* to make a plural noun.

EXAMPLES	Singular	Plural
	city	cities
	story	stories
	penny	pennies

Activity B   Make two columns on your paper. Write the following twelve nouns in column 1. Then write the plural of each noun in column 2.

1) fly

2) toy

3) valley

4) activity

5) turkey

6) delay

7) bully

8) salary

9) cry

10) copy

11) army

12) candy

Nouns Ending With *-f* or *-fe*

Some singular nouns end with *-f* or *-fe*. Sometimes you just add *-s* to make a plural noun. At other times, you must change the *f* to *v* and add *-s* or *-es*. How can you tell what to do? Try pronouncing the plural noun carefully. Listen for the *f* or *v* sound.

EXAMPLES	Singular	Plural
	roof	roofs
	belief	beliefs
	leaf	leaves
	wife	wives

Activity C Read each singular noun below. Then say its plural form aloud. Write the correct plural on your paper.

1) calf

2) thief

3) life

4) knife

5) chief

6) cliff

7) wolf

8) giraffe

9) shelf

10) chef

Nouns Ending With -o

A few nouns end with the letter *o*. If there is a vowel before the *o*, just add -*s* to make a plural noun.

EXAMPLES	Singular	Plural
	radio	radios
	stereo	stereos
	tattoo	tattoos

If a singular noun ends with a consonant before the letter *o*, you usually add -*es* to make a plural.

EXAMPLES	Singular	Plural
	potato	potatoes
	echo	echoes
	veto	vetoes
	tomato	tomatoes

With musical terms, just add -*s* to form the plural.

EXAMPLES	Singular	Plural
	piano	pianos
	solo	solos
	banjo	banjos

Activity D   Complete each sentence with the plural form of the bold noun. Write the plural on your paper.

1) Amanda has tried the **shampoo** in the pink bottle. Are some _____ better than others?

2) Which music **video** do you like? Some of the _____ are boring.

3) The girls went to the **rodeo**. How many _____ have you seen?

4) Laura is eating a baked **potato**. Mike ordered mashed _____.

5) We shouted and listened to our **echo**. The tunnel was great for _____!

6) Mike plays the **banjo**. He has two _____.

Irregular Plural Nouns

Some plural nouns are irregular. An irregular plural noun does not form its plural with the usual *-s* or *-es*. Study the following irregular plural nouns.

Singular	Plural	Singular	Plural
child	children	tooth	teeth
man	men	goose	geese
woman	women	mouse	mice
foot	feet		

Activity E   Choose four of the plural nouns from the list above. Write each one in a separate sentence on your paper.

Sometimes the singular and plural forms of the noun are the same. Here is a list of nouns that do not change their spellings.

Singular	Plural	Singular	Plural
one deer	several deer	one fish	a few fish
one sheep	many sheep	a trout	many trout
one moose	two moose		

Activity F   Number your paper from 1 to 4. Read each sentence below. If the sentence has no errors, write *Correct* after the number. If the sentence has an error, rewrite the sentence.

1) The man and his dog herded the sheeps into the pen.
2) The pet store sells tropical fish.
3) Do mooses live in Maine?
4) The fisherman caught a dozen trout during the afternoon.

Activity G   Review the proper spelling of plurals. Find one mistake in each sentence. Rewrite the word correctly.

1) Springfield has fifteen churchs.
2) Around Springfield are several valleyes.
3) There are also mountaines.
4) In the fall the leafs on the trees all turn to red and gold.
5) People often see deers in the hills.
6) Springfield parents care about their childrens.
7) Farms around Springfield are famous for their potatos.
8) The people's lifes in Springfield are usually pleasant.

Plurals of Proper Nouns

You may want to write the plural of a proper noun such as a family name. Here are rules for writing the plurals of proper nouns.

1. Add *-s* or *-es* to make a name plural.

> **EXAMPLES** Ms. O'Hara and her family the O'Haras
> Coach Jones and his family the Joneses
> Laura Gonzales and her family the Gonzaleses

2. If a name ends with a consonant before the letter *y*, do NOT change the *y* to *i*.

> **EXAMPLES** Sophie Stansky invited all the Stanskys to a party.
> Kelly Takemura and Kelly Harte are in our class;
> our class has two Kellys.

3. Do NOT use an apostrophe to make a plural. Use an apostrophe only to make a possessive.

> **EXAMPLES** **Plural Proper Nouns**
> the Moyerses   the O'Haras
> The Ruizes   the Palombos
>
> **Singular Possessive Proper Nouns**
> James's hat   Kelly's book   Mr. Takemura's family
>
> **Plural Possessive Proper Nouns**
> the Joneses' car   the Takemuras' house

Activity H   Find the error in each sentence below and at the top of the next page. Write the proper noun correctly on your paper.

1) John Adams and other Adams' were famous in American history.

2) The Lowrys have six Mary's in their family.

3) Have you ever eaten at the Nucci's restaurant?

4) The Gonzaleses' have lived in Texas for more than 100 years.

5) Charles Dickens books are still popular.

6) Choon-Cho stayed with the Kim's when she came from Korea.

Activity I   Write the plural of each family name in a sentence on your paper. Then write the plural possessive of each family name in a sentence.

Example   The Carters came to dinner last Sunday.
Have you seen the Carters' new car?

1) Chang

2) Ruiz

3) Williams

4) Corelli

Plurals of Letters and Numbers

An apostrophe is not used to make a plural. If a plural letter would be confusing without an apostrophe, use one to make the letter plural.

  How many *s*'s are in Mississippi?
Oona's name has two *o*'s in it.
Children learn their ABCs.

When making a plural with a number, use no apostrophe.

  The Vietnam War was fought in the 1960s.
When were Boeing 727s first made?

Activity J   Write five sentences. Use a plural number or letter in each sentence.

Plural nouns name more than one person, place, thing, or idea. Pay attention to plural nouns in your writing. Make sure that you have spelled them correctly. Remember these points.

- With most nouns, add -*s* or -*es* to make a plural.
- If a singular noun ends with a consonant followed by *y*, change the *y* to *i* before adding -*es*.
- If a singular noun ends with -*f* or -*fe*, you may need to form a plural that ends with -*ves*.
- Do not add -*s* or -*es* to form the plural of an irregular noun.
- Do not use an apostrophe when writing plurals of proper names.
- Use an apostrophe to write the plural of a letter if it would be confusing without one.
- Do not use an apostrophe to write a plural number.

Part A Find the one spelling error in each sentence below. Write the word correctly on your paper.

1) There are many beautiful beachs in these states.
2) Mike and Derek left their watchs in their lockers.
3) Why are the students' playing their radios in class?
4) These glass are filled with berries.
5) Will taxes rise in the cityes?
6) Put the potatoes on the shelfs.
7) We heard the cries of the wolfs.
8) The class read three playes and two stories.
9) The leafs on these bushes are gold and red.
10) Each of these dancers has two left foot.
11) Elana wears braces to straighten her teeths.
12) The Corellis' give two parties a year.
13) The Ostrowskys lived in three countrys in the 1980s.
14) Three deers wandered through the Nguyens' yard.
15) The Vanderbilts and the Astors were wealthy familys.

Part B Write one or two sentences with each pair of nouns.

1) goose, geese   3) flash, flashes   5) fly, flies
2) life, lives   4) Wilson's, Wilsons

Words with *ie* or *ei* may confuse spellers. How can you tell which letter to put first? Try memorizing this verse:

> Put *i* before *e*
> Except after *c*
> Or when sounded like *A*
> As in *neighbor* and *weigh*.

EXAMPLES   "i before e"—ach**ie**ve, bel**ie**ve, th**ie**f
"except after c"—rec**ei**ve, c**ei**ling, dec**ei**t
"Or when sounded like A"—n**ei**ghbor, w**ei**gh, fr**ei**ght

Activity A   Look at each pair of words below. Think about the verse above. Decide which word is spelled correctly. Copy the correct spelling on your paper.

1) chief, cheif

2) reins, riens

3) sliegh, sleigh

4) releif, relief

5) niece, neice

6) peice, piece

7) receipt, reciept

8) thieves, theives

9) freind, friend

10) greif, grief

11) acheive, achieve

12) cieling, ceiling

13) beleive, believe

14) feild, field

15) conceited, concieted

16) freight, frieght

17) reign, riegn

18) releived, relieved

19) shriek, shreik

20) diesel, deisel

Unfortunately, some words do not follow the pattern in the verse. You can learn these exceptions. Look at each word, spell it aloud, and write it. The correct spellings will become familiar to you.

Exceptions

either	science
neither	conscience
height	ancient
seize	
weird	
foreign	
leisure	
protein	
caffeine	

Activity B   Look over the 12 words in the list of exceptions. Decide which one fits best in each sentence below. Write the word on your paper.

1) Mr. O'Hara does not like coffee with _____ in it.

2) Choose _____ the black shoes or the white shoes.

3) "That noise sounded _____!" whispered Mike. "I'm scared!"

4) Ruben's _____ is five feet nine inches.

5) Immigrants come to the United States from _____ countries.

6) The Egyptians built pyramids in _____ times.

7) Do the workers have enough time for _____ activities?

8) Athletes must eat foods that have _____.

9) Biology and geology are _____ subjects.

10) _____ Valerie nor her brother has been on a plane.

11) The police tried to _____ the thief.

12) The thief's _____ bothered him, so he returned the money.

When you are trying to decide whether to spell a word with *ie* or *ei*, remember the verse about using those letters. Also make yourself familiar with spellings that are exceptions to the rule.

Part A   Read the sentences. Find the words with *ie* or *ei*. Decide whether each one is spelled correctly. Write all the words correctly on your paper.

1) "I beleive that waiting tables is the hardest job in the world," said Loreen. "What a relief to sit down at last!"

2) Footprints were on the cieling. Someone had been up to mischief!

3) Amanda won an award for acheivement. When her name was announced, she shrieked loudly.

4) The child's weight was forty pounds. Her hieght was forty inches.

5) The driver did not yeild to the cars on the highway. The driver received a ticket.

Part B   Write one or two sentences on your paper using each pair of words below. You do not have to match the order shown.

1) either, conscience
2) shield, piece
3) foreign, ancient
4) chief, niece
5) fierce, seize
6) freight, weigh
7) believe, thieves
8) weird, science
9) friend, grief
10) briefly, deceived

Many words have endings added to them. You may need to make a spelling change in the word before you add the ending. For example, you may need to double the final consonant. Suppose that you are describing what a frog did. If you write *hoped* when you mean *hopped*, your readers will be confused.

Look at these words:

hop	big	slam	shut	wet

These words have three things in common.

1. They all have just one syllable.
2. They all end in just one consonant.
3. They all have just one vowel before the final consonant.

Study this rule. It tells you when to double a final consonant.

- Double the final consonant of a word before adding an ending if:
  — the word has just one syllable,
  — the word has one final consonant, and
  — the word has one vowel before the final consonant.

Here are some endings that begin with vowels:

-ing	-ed	-er	-est	-y	-ist

EXAMPLES **Words in Which the Final Consonant Is Doubled:**

hop + ed = hopped   shut + ing = shutting
big + er = bigger   wet + est = wettest
slam + ed = slammed   pin + ed = pinned
mud + y = muddy   drug + ist = druggist

Words in Which the Final Consonant is NOT Doubled:

sweet + er = sweeter   (*Two* vowels come before the final consonant.)

jump + ed = jumped   (*Two* consonants come at the end.)

sad + ly = sadly   (The ending begins with a *consonant*.)

Activity A   Double the final consonant before adding each ending below. Write the new word in a sentence.

1) ship + ed

2) big + est

3) hop + ing

4) hem + ed

5) plan + er

Activity B   The final consonant should be doubled in only some of the words below. Add the ending to each word. Write the new word on your paper.

1) sharp + er

2) sweet + er

3) chop + ed

4) sun + y

5) art + ist

6) grab + ed

7) star + y

8) dig + ing

9) mad + ly

10) hurt + ing

Activity C   Find the one misspelled word in each sentence below. Write the sentence correctly on your paper.

1) The frog hoped into the water and made a plopping noise.

2) Someone has been digging in the mudy pond.

3) Was Derek a winer at the track meet?

4) The cook stired the soup and added salt.

5) The trail ended, and we steped into the clearing.

Two-Syllable Words

Sometimes you will need to double the final consonant in a two-syllable word. Look at these two-syllable words:

begin	forgot	control

These words have three things in common.

1. They all end in just one consonant.

2. They all have just one vowel before the final consonant.

3. The second syllable is stressed, or spoken with greater force than the first syllable.

Here is the rule to follow for doubling the final consonant in words of more than one syllable.

- If the final syllable is stressed and has just one vowel before one final consonant, double that final consonant before an ending that begins with a vowel.

EXAMPLES

Words in Which the Final Consonant Is Doubled:
begin + er   = beginner
control + ed = controlled
forget + ing = forgetting

Words in Which the Final Consonant Is NOT Doubled:

return + ed = returned	(The final syllable, *turn*, ends in *two* consonants.)
travel + er = traveler	(The final syllable, *el*, is not stressed.)
repeat + ed = repeated	(*Two* vowels come before the final consonant.)
forget + ful = forgetful	(The ending begins with a *consonant*.)

Activity D Look at each pair of words below. Decide which word is spelled correctly. Copy the correct spelling on your paper.

1) offering, offerring

2) controller, controler

3) difference, differrence

4) referral, referal

5) equipped, equiped

6) equippment, equipment

7) beginning, begining

8) piloted, pilotted

Look carefully at words with endings. Make sure that you have doubled final consonants when needed. Make sure that you have not doubled final consonants unless needed. Here are the two rules to follow.

- When a word has just one syllable, one final consonant, and one vowel before that consonant, double the final consonant before an ending that begins with a vowel.
  Example   big + er = bigger

- In a two-syllable word, if the final syllable is stressed and has just one vowel before one final consonant, double that final consonant before an ending that begins with a vowel.
  Example   begin + er = beginner

Part A   Put each word and ending together. Write the new word on your paper.

1) color + ful
2) admit + ed
3) swim + er
4) run + ing
5) hop + ed
6) open + ed
7) fat + est
8) sit + ing
9) wait + er
10) hand + y
11) nut + y
12) great + est
13) limit + ed
14) hot + est
15) begin + ing
16) occur + ence
17) permit + ed
18) bat + er
19) number + ed
20) refer + ing

Part B   Look at each pair of words below. Decide which word is spelled correctly. Write a sentence with the correctly spelled word.

1) choper, chopper
2) prefered, preferred
3) patroling, patrolling
4) hiting, hitting
5) sadest, saddest

Dropping the Final -e

Many words have endings added to them. You may need to make a spelling change in the word before you add the ending. For example, you may need to drop a silent final -*e*. Or you may need to keep a silent final -*e*.

These two rules will help you decide how to add endings to words that have a silent final -*e*.

1. Keep the silent -*e* before an ending that begins with a consonant.

> **EXAMPLES**   safe + ly = safely
> use + ful = useful
> excite + ment = excitement

2. Drop the silent -*e* before an ending that begins with a vowel.

> **EXAMPLES**   take + ing = taking
> noise + y = noisy
> receive + ed = received

Activity A   Put each word and ending together. Write the new word on your paper.

1) strange + ly

2) safe + ty

3) believe + able

4) arrange + ing

5) choose + ing

6) hope + ed

7) wiggle + ing

8) hope + ful

9) write + ing

10) surprise + ing

11) refuse + al

12) bake + er

Activity B   Find the one misspelled word in each sentence below. Write it correctly on your paper.

1) We are hopeing that Keisha will be pleased with the gift.

2) I am writeing to inform you that I am changing my address.

3) The detectives were puzzleing over the confusing clues.

4) The roller coaster is the most exciting ride at any amusment park.

5) After separating the egg whites and yolks, whip each part separatly.

6) Please be carful when arranging those flowers.

7) The diver has a wirey build.

8) "The car makes a noisy, whineing sound," said the owner.

9) The littlest child has an adoreable smile.

10) Smokeing is no longer allowed in many offices.

Activity C   Add the ending *-ing* to each word below. Write the new word in a sentence.

1) come

2) admire

3) care

4) dance

5) divide

6) argue

7) circle

8) apologize

9) compare

10) chase

Many words end in silent -*e*. Remember to drop the -*e* before an ending IF that ending begins with a vowel.

Part A   Add each ending to the word shown. Write the new words on your paper.

1) taste + ful
   taste + y

2) advertise + ment
   advertise + ing

3) excite + ing
   excite + ment

4) care + less
   care + ing

5) use + ing
   use + ful

6) arrange + ment
   arrange + er

7) debate + able
   debate + ing

8) scare + y
   scare + ing

9) trouble + ing
   trouble + some

10) tickle + ish
    tickle + er

Part B   Find five spelling errors in the passage below. Write each word correctly on your paper.

The Tennis Match
by Mike Kaplan

My friend, Derek Corelli, and I had been practiceing for several weeks. At first, we were mostly chaseing the ball around. Finally, we decided that we were good enough to make a challenge. There was a lot of excitement in Springfield as the news got around. That day we saw several of our friends arriveing to watch us play.

To make a long story short, we were not exactly blazeing the ball. No one confusd us with Pete Sampras and Andre Agassi.

"It's hard to play well with a tree growing in the middle of the court," Derek complained to me after we lost 6–0, 6–0.

"Oh, yeah!" I said. "Well, most people I know need to have their rackets restrung from time to time. You need to have your racket rewooded!"

Some words are misspelled more often than other words. These spelling demons may be troublesome to you, too. The way to learn spelling demons is to practice writing them correctly again and again.

Read this list of fifty commonly misspelled words.

1) acquaint	**18)** experience	**35)** pleasant
2) across	**19)** false	**36)** privilege
3) athletic	**20)** February	**37)** realize
4) beautiful	**21)** film	**38)** recommend
5) benefit	**22)** finally	**39)** secretary
6) business	**23)** forty	**40)** separate
7) character	**24)** government	**41)** similar
8) clothes	**25)** grammar	**42)** since
9) committee	**26)** immediately	**43)** speech
10) decision	**27)** interesting	**44)** surprise
11) definite	**28)** knowledge	**45)** thorough
12) describe	**29)** library	**46)** together
13) description	**30)** minute	**47)** true
14) different	**31)** necessary	**48)** usually
15) disappear	**32)** ninety	**49)** Wednesday
16) disappoint	**33)** occasion	**50)** which
17) doctor	**34)** once	

Activity A Study the list above.

1) Say each word aloud. Cover the word with your hand. Spell it aloud. Check your spelling.

2) Then have someone else read aloud each word on the list. Write each word on your paper.

3) Check to see which words you misspelled. Cross out each misspelled word and write it correctly three times.

Activity B Find the one misspelled word in each sentence below. Write the word correctly on your paper.

1) You can add to your knowledge by finding interesting books in the libary.

2) "It is my privlege to recommend Keisha for committee secretary," said Loreen.

3) Mr. Corelli finaly turned forty in February.

4) Derek has certainly benefited from his atheletic efforts.

5) "On which occasion did you make a fasle statement?" the lawyer asked the witness.

6) The docter made a thorough examination of the ninety-year-old man.

7) The characters in this flim wore beautiful clothes.

8) The federal government is divided into seperate branches.

9) Is your decision definate, or could you change your mind at the last minute?

10) It is absolutely necessary for a secretary to have knowlege of grammar and spelling rules.

11) How did the writer descibe the different characters?

12) Let me aquaint you with the business owners across the hall.

13) The decision is not a surprise, but it still disapoints us.

14) Can you give a description of the pleasant experience you had Wednesday?

15) The character in the film gave a speech that lasted one minite.

Lesson 8 Review

The fifty words in this lesson are difficult for many people to spell. It helps to pronounce each word carefully before writing it. With study and practice, you can learn to spell these words correctly.

Part A   Read both spellings of the ten words listed below. Write the correct spelling of each word on your paper.

1) accrost, across

2) benifit, benefit

3) separate, seperate

4) nessary, necessary

5) togehter, together

6) February, Febuary

7) atheletic, athletic

8) libary, library

9) simler, similar

10) usually, usally

Part B   Look over the list of fifty words. Choose ten that are hard for you to spell. Write each one in a sentence on your paper.

Part A   Choose the word in parentheses that correctly completes the sentence. Write the word on your paper.

1) The players threw (there, their) hats into the air.

2) The workers are not (quiet, quite) done paving the road.

3) One shoe feels tight, and the other feels (lose, loose).

4) We were busy, so time (past, passed) quickly.

5) Drive (two, to) or three blocks north on Main Street.

6) Will people follow good (advice, advise)?

7) Please be (carful, careful) near a hot stove.

8) The dog has a white spot on (it's, its) back.

9) (Theirs, There's) more than one way to reach our house.

10) "Is that (your, you're) scarf or mine?" Amanda asked Laura.

11) A woodworker smoothes a shelf by (planning, planing) it.

12) The general (pined, pinned) the medal on the war hero.

13) Two rabbits were (hoping, hopping) quickly across the road.

14) "Unbelievable!" the man said, (staring, starring) wide-eyed at the scene.

15) Do (caned, canned) peas taste as good as fresh ones?

Part B   Each sentence below and at the top of the next page contains at least one spelling error. Rewrite each sentence on your paper. Make sure that all words are spelled correctly.

1) The business owner finaly reached a desion on Wenesday.

2) The guideance councilor spoke to the school principal.

3) "Were already through with a week's work," said the commitee members.

4) State governments are usally located in the capitol cityes.

5) The whether today is effecting the gooses strangely.

6) Its true that male foxs are careing fathers of there families.

7) The buses stoped runing last Febuary.

8) I read a library book about the lifes of sports heroes.

9) It's likly that the potatos are on the shelfs.

10) "I cant beleive how many spelling errors your makeing!" Mr. Martin repeatted to all his class.

Part C   Write a sentence with each pair of words below. You do not have to match the order shown.

1) since, February

2) necessary, together

3) speeches, exciting

4) preferred, beginner

5) hottest, biggest

6) you're, your

7) they're, their

8) weird, receiving

9) piece, peaceful

10) woman, women

Test Taking Tip   To prepare for a test, study in short sessions rather than one long session. In the week before the test, spend time each evening reviewing your notes.

Chapter 5

Writing Complete Sentences

Think about the last conversation you had with someone. Can you remember what each of you said? It is likely that neither of you spoke in complete sentences. Speakers can usually understand each other even when their sentences are incomplete or run together.

Writing, however, is not the same as speaking. When you write, you need to pay close attention to your sentences. If your sentences are incomplete, your readers may be puzzled. If your sentences run together, your readers may be lost.

You have learned that a sentence is a group of words containing a subject and a verb and expressing a complete idea. In Chapter 5, you will learn to look for and fix two common sentence errors that can confuse readers.

Goals for Learning

▶ To recognize and fix run-on sentences
▶ To recognize and fix sentence fragments

Run-on sentence

Two or more complete ideas that are not connected correctly. (I have read that book many times I'll read it again, it is my favorite and you'll like it too.)

When a sentence seems to run on without coming to a stop, it is called a **run-on sentence**. A run-on sentence has too many ideas in it. The ideas should be clearly separated.

Before you can fix run-on errors, you need to know what they look like. A run-on sentence is often made of two or more sentences with no punctuation between them.

> **EXAMPLE**   Derek and Mike like tennis they play as often as they can.

The easiest way to correct a run-on sentence is to split it into separate sentences. Review the rules for writing a sentence.

1. Capitalize the first word in a sentence.

2. End a sentence with the correct punctuation mark. A period is the most common end punctuation mark. The only other end marks are the question mark and the exclamation point.

3. Do not end a sentence with a comma.

Here is the easiest way to fix the run-on sentence shown in the example above.

> **EXAMPLE**   Derek and Mike like tennis. They play as often as they can.

Activity A   Each group of words below is a run-on sentence. Decide where the first idea ends and the second idea begins. Rewrite the ideas in two correct sentences on your paper. Check for correct capitalization and end punctuation.

1) Do you have an extra tennis racket mine is lost.

2) Meet me at the courts after school we can play for an hour before dark.

3) Derek and Mike practiced for several days then they challenged two players to a tennis match and lost.

Activity B   Each group of words below is a run-on sentence containing three ideas. Find the beginning and the end of each complete thought. Write the three sentences on your paper. Use capital letters and end punctuation correctly.

Example   Run-on:
Thank you for talking with me on the phone last week my job application is enclosed I look forward to meeting with you

Three sentences:
Thank you for talking with me on the phone last week.
My job application is enclosed.
I look forward to meeting with you.

1) Amanda stayed up too late last night she was reading an interesting book all day she kept yawning

2) Mike has set up another tennis match he thinks that he and Derek will win Derek is not so sure

3) last year Derek wanted to be a diesel mechanic now he likes sports he is thinking about becoming a physical education teacher

4) the tennis match was held at noon on Saturday Mike and Derek lost again Derek decided to stick to track

5) Springfield Senior High has a weight room every day Laura goes there for an hour she feels strong and fit

6) the county track meet will be held next week Derek wants to set a new record everyone hopes that he will win

Connecting Ideas

Another kind of run-on sentence is made of two or more sentences separated with commas. Do not separate two sentences with a comma. This kind of error is sometimes called a comma fault. Use an end punctuation mark—not a comma—to end a sentence.

EXAMPLES	**Run-on Sentence With Comma Fault** Coach Jones is proud of Derek, he hopes that Derek will become county champion. **Corrected Sentences** Coach Jones is proud of Derek. He hopes that Derek will become county champion.

Sometimes you may want to show the connection between two related ideas. Turn your run-on sentence into a compound sentence. The two ideas in a compound sentence are separated by a comma followed by a **conjunction**. Notice the conjunction *and* in the compound sentence below.

Conjunction

A word used to connect words or phrases or to combine complete ideas in sentences (and, or, but).

EXAMPLES	**Run-on Sentence With Comma Fault** Coach Jones is proud of Derek, he hopes that Derek will become county champion. **Corrected Compound Sentence** Coach Jones is proud of Derek, and he hopes that Derek will become county champion.

Activity C   Read each group of words below. Decide whether each group is a correct sentence or a run-on sentence. Write *Correct* or *Run-on* as your answer on your paper.

1) Mike went to the weight room with Derek, and they both worked out.

2) One afternoon Derek and Mike met Laura in the weight room, she was working out, too.

3) A track meet is exciting and suspenseful, have you ever gone to one?

4) Derek's friends want to go to the county meet, and they plan to cheer from the stands.

5) Some people enjoy team sports, and others like to work out by themselves.

6) Tennis is played with rackets and a ball, what other sport uses rackets?

Activity D   Each run-on sentence below has a comma fault. Decide how to fix the problem. You may decide to separate the ideas into two complete sentences. If the ideas seem related, add the conjunction *and* after the comma. Rewrite the sentences on your paper.

1) What will you do during your week off, please come to visit us.

2) The main character in this book is a sixteen-year-old boy, he dreams of becoming a fighter.

3) The weight room will be open after school until five, no one will be admitted without permission.

4) The detective tries to figure out who committed the crime, the reader already knows who did it.

5) Derek started out running the mile, then he switched to sprinting.

6) My parents arrived in the United States in 1975, I was born six years later.

Using Conjunctions Correctly

Another kind of run-on sentence is made with two or more sentences connected with *ands*. Do not use *ands* to connect sentences that should be separated.

EXAMPLES

Run-on Sentence With Too Many ands
The game last Saturday was Johnson's greatest and he'll probably bring the Foxes into the championship and the fans can't wait to see this guy make another touchdown.

Corrected Sentences
The game last Saturday was Johnson's greatest! He'll probably bring the Foxes into the championship. The fans can't wait to see this guy make another touchdown.

Activity E   Read the paragraph below. Decide where each complete idea begins and ends. Look for four complete sentences. Write the sentences on your paper. Make sure to use capital letters and end punctuation correctly.

My Favorite Song
by Laura Gonzales

   Sometimes a song can have a strong effect on a listener and my eyes always fill up with tears when I hear "From Out of My Heart" and it is so powerful and listening to it makes me want to write a sad song, too.

Write your complete ideas as separate sentences. Check your work for run-on sentences, and fix them.

- Begin each sentence with a capital letter. End it with a period, a question mark, or an exclamation point.

- Do not use a comma to separate complete ideas. Fix a comma fault by writing separate sentences. If the ideas are related, make a compound sentence with a comma and a conjunction.

- Avoid connecting separate ideas with *ands*. Write separate sentences instead.

Part A   Read each group of words below. Number your paper from 1 to 5. If the group of words is correct, write *Correct* as your answer. If the group of words is a run-on sentence, rewrite it so that it is correct. There may be more than one way to correct a run-on sentence.

1) Mike went to the tennis courts alone, he practiced his serve.

2) Soon he and Derek would make another challenge, and the next time they would win.

3) Eat at Anna's Restaurant, the pizza is perfect, the sauces are super!

4) I purchased a toaster oven at Riley's Discount Store last November it stopped working last week my sales slip is enclosed.

5) There are too many ideas in a run-on sentence the ideas need to be separated.

Part B   Choose any topic that interests you. Write five sentences about that topic. Include at least one compound sentence that uses *and*. Do not write any run-on sentences.

Fragment

A group of words that does not express a complete thought; a phrase or clause incorrectly treated as a sentence.

You have learned that a sentence is a group of words containing a subject and a verb and expressing a complete idea. If the subject or the verb is missing, the sentence is a **fragment**. It fails to express a complete idea. Any group of words that does not express a complete idea is a fragment. Fragments may confuse your readers.

Each fragment below begins with a capital letter and ends with a period. It only looks like a sentence, however. It does not express a complete thought. Notice how each fragment is turned into a complete sentence.

EXAMPLES

Fragment:	Going to the track meet.
Sentence:	Derek is going to the track meet.
Fragment:	The team from Springfield.
Sentence:	The team from Springfield has strong runners.
Fragment:	Because Derek is so fast.
Sentence:	Because Derek is so fast, he may win his race.

Activity A   Read each group of words below. Decide whether each group is a correct sentence or a fragment. Write *Sentence* or *Fragment* as your answer on your paper.

1) Running laps around the track after school.

2) Most of the other members of the track team.

3) A challenging race.

4) Anyone can enjoy running.

5) You should learn to stretch first.

6) Where there are few cars.

Activity B   Make all of the sentence fragments in Activity A into complete sentences. Add words to make each group of words express a complete thought. Underline your added words.

Two Parts of a Sentence

The subject of a sentence is the person, place, thing, or idea that a sentence tells about. Every sentence needs a subject. Look at the bold subject in each example sentence.

> **EXAMPLES**
>
> **The gas station** is open.
>
> **Derek and Ms. Lentz** have been working there.
>
> **He** pumps gas.
>
> **She** fixes cars.

Predicate

The part of a sentence that tells something about the subject; it always contains a verb.

Every sentence also needs a **predicate**. The predicate tells what the subject is or does. Look at the bold predicate in each example sentence.

> **EXAMPLES**
>
> The gas station **is open**. (The verb is *is*.)
>
> Derek and Ms. Lentz **have been working there**. (The verb is *have been working*.)
>
> He **pumps gas**. (The verb is *pumps*.)
>
> She **fixes cars**. (The verb is *fixes*.)

Activity C   Each group of words below is a sentence fragment. Either a subject or a predicate is missing. Decide what part is missing. Then add words to turn the fragment into a complete sentence. Write the complete sentences on your paper. Underline your added words.

1) Enjoys working on cars.

2) Works part-time at the gas station.

3) The owner of the gas station.

4) A job at the gas station.

5) Greeted the customers with a smile.

6) Asked about checking the oil.

7) The gas station on the next corner.

8) The driver of a blue van.

Incomplete Ideas

A sentence fragment is any incomplete expression. It leaves the reader wondering *who? what? what about it?* Any group of words may be a sentence fragment. Here are more examples of sentence fragments. Compare each fragment with the complete sentence below it.

EXAMPLES	Fragment:	To go to work.
	Sentence:	It was time to go to work.
	Fragment:	On the bus.
	Sentence:	Everyone rode on the bus.
	Fragment:	When the bus broke down.
	Sentence:	The riders climbed out when the bus broke down.

Look carefully at any sentence that begins with a word such as *because, when, where, since, that, which, or, if, to, for, from,* or *with.* Make sure that you have written a complete idea.

Activity D   Decide whether each group of words below is a complete sentence or a fragment. If it is a sentence, write *Sentence* on your paper. If it is a fragment, add words to make it complete. Write the new sentence correctly.

1) Because it is raining, the game is postponed.

2) With luck and hard work.

3) To be the best at everything.

4) When Derek runs.

5) Or a job building houses on Belmont Street.

6) From Chicago, Detroit, and Cleveland.

7) Because the math course was challenging.

8) If you come to town, please call.

9) That had ever been seen before.

10) Where young people can meet.

Activity E Find the fragments below. Correct them. You may join the fragment with the rest of the sentence. You may add words to turn the fragment into a complete sentence. Write your new sentences on your paper.

Examples:

Fragment: Amanda goes to dancing class. With her mother.

Sentence: Amanda goes to dancing class with her mother.

Sentences: Amanda goes to dancing class. She tap dances with her mother.

1) On a sunny day. Amanda and Laura decided to go to an amusement park.

2) They asked Mike and Derek. To come along.

3) The friends had never been to this park. Which had many thrilling rides.

4) The park was crowded. With long lines of people.

5) Because they knew they would enjoy crashing into one another. They headed for the bumper cars

6) They took a boat ride. On the lake.

7) The four friends stood in line for the roller coaster. For an hour.

8) When it was time to get on. Derek changed his mind.

9) Laura, Mike, and Amanda begged him. To give it a try.

10) The roller coaster climbed. Derek watched it. From his spot on the ground.

Answering Questions With Complete Sentences

Speakers often use sentence fragments to answer questions. The person who asks the question usually understands the fragment answer. Compare the fragment answer with the sentence answer in each example below.

EXAMPLES

Question:	What do you want for lunch?
Fragment answer:	A hot dog.
Sentence answer:	I would like a hot dog.
Question:	Which ride did you like best?
Fragment answer:	The roller coaster.
Sentence answer:	The roller coaster was my favorite ride.
Question:	Why did you like the roller coaster best?
Fragment answer:	Because I enjoy being scared.
Sentence answer:	I liked the roller coaster because I enjoy being scared.

An answer that is a sentence fragment does not make sense unless the reader knows the question.

Activity F Answer these questions in complete sentences. The answers should make sense to a reader who does not know what the question is. Do not answer question 10 with just *yes* or *no*.

1) What is your full name?

2) Where were you born?

3) How old are you?

4) What school do you attend?

5) Where is the school located?

6) What is the name of the town or city where you live?

7) How long have you lived there?

8) What is your favorite television program?

9) Why do you like that program?

10) Are all of these answers complete sentences?

Check your writing for sentence fragments. Make sure that each sentence expresses a complete idea. To fix a fragment, you may need to join it to another sentence. You may need to add words to the fragment to turn it into a complete sentence.

Part A   Read each group of words carefully. Decide whether the words express a complete idea. Write either *Sentence* or *Fragment* as your answer on your paper.

1) The trip to the amusement park.

2) Mike, Derek, Laura, and Amanda went together.

3) "The next time I go there."

4) "I might try the roller coaster," said Derek.

5) Mike had eaten five hot dogs.

6) While he was at the park.

7) Derek refused to eat one.

8) He said they tasted terrible.

9) Is watching his diet carefully.

10) When Derek is in training.

Part B   Choose any experience you have had. Write five sentences about that experience. Begin one of the sentences with the word *When*. Check your work to make sure that all of your sentences are complete.

Part A   Answer each of these questions with a complete sentence.

1) What is a run-on sentence?

2) What is one way to fix a run-on sentence?

3) What must come at the end of every sentence?

4) Why should a writer watch out for fragments?

5) What is one way to recognize a sentence fragment?

Part B   Read each group of words below. Decide whether each group is a correct sentence or a run-on sentence. Write *Correct* or *Run-on* on your paper. If the sentence is a run-on, rewrite it to make it correct.

1) Victor has a new interest he is learning to cook.

2) Victor's friends can't believe that he wants to spend his time reading cookbooks and chopping vegetables.

3) I tasted Victor's peanut stew, it was delicious!

4) Cooking takes practice, it requires patience.

5) Victor says that food should taste good, and it should look good, too.

Part C   Read each group of words below. Decide whether each group is a correct sentence or a fragment. Write *Correct* or *Fragment* on your paper. If the sentence is a fragment, rewrite it to make it correct.

1) Played against a stronger team.

2) Most of the other basketball players.

3) A hard game to play well.

4) Anyone can play basketball.

5) You should learn to pass the ball.

Part D Read each group of words below. Decide whether it is a run-on sentence or a sentence fragment. Write *Run-on* or *Fragment* on your paper. Then show how you would correct the problem. Write the complete sentences on your paper.

1) I was in the stands with Derek's other friends it was Saturday morning and we all waited for Derek's first race to begin.

2) Derek had trained hard, we were sure he would win.

3) For the 200-meter run, which is one of the fastest of all track-and-field events.

4) Need to burst out like lightning.

5) It's all over in less than half a minute, it's amazingly fast!

6) All the runners exploded out of the blocks, we screamed until we were hoarse.

7) Two runners flew across the ribbon together one of them was Derek.

8) Was first?

9) Our friend, Derek Corelli, we felt so proud to know him.

10) With a trophy to put on his shelf.

Part E Read the paragraph below. Find the sentence errors. Rewrite the paragraph as five sentences on your paper.

> Laura enjoys singing rounds, she taught her niece and nephew to sing "Row, Row, Row Your Boat" and later the three of them sang "Todos los Pollitos" when everyone sang a different line. All three voices blended together well and several listeners clapped

Test Taking Tip When you are reading a test question, pay attention to words that are emphasized in bold type or in capital letters. Those words will help you decide how best to answer the question.

Chapter

6

Making Each Sentence Count

Do you know someone who tells a joke or a story well? That person knows how to hold an audience's attention. A skillful speaker uses just the right words to help listeners picture actions and understand ideas. A skillful speaker makes every sentence count.

When you write, you try to hold your readers' attention, too. You want them to form sharp pictures in their minds. You want them to understand your message clearly.

In this chapter, you will learn how to choose just the right words. You will learn how to make every sentence count.

Goals for Learning

▶ To improve sentences by adding adjectives, adverbs, and prepositional phrases

▶ To combine short, choppy sentences and show clear connections among ideas

▶ To build variety into sentences

Modifier

A word that describes another word in a sentence.

The words in a sentence all have jobs. The main job of some words is to describe, or tell about, other words. Describing words give more information about the other words. Because the describing words change, or modify, meaning, they are also called **modifiers**.

You have learned that an adjective describes a noun or pronoun. An adjective tells how many, what kind, or which ones. Look at the bold adjectives in each list below. Think about the question each one answers.

> **EXAMPLES**   *How many?*
> **one** dog, **few** animals, **nineteen** students
>
> *What kind?*
> **furry** dogs, **extinct** dinosaurs, **curious** students
>
> *Which ones?*
> **those** dogs, **the** animals, **other** friends

Adjectives add details to sentences. Adjectives often appear before the words they modify. Read the sentences below. The adjectives are bold. In the first example sentence, adjectives come before the nouns *man, glass, lemonade,* and *gulps.* In the second example sentence, adjectives come before the nouns *kitten* and *yarn.*

> **EXAMPLES**   **The thirsty** man drank **a tall** glass of **pink** lemonade in **four** gulps.
>
> **A fuzzy black** kitten had wrapped itself in **thick yellow** yarn.

Activity A   Think of an adjective that could describe each noun below. Write the adjective on your paper.

1) _____ tree

2) _____ teachers

3) _____ haircut

4) _____ motorcycle

5) _____ elephants

You may write sentences in which an adjective does not come before the noun. The adjective still modifies the noun, but it comes after the verb. An adjective often follows a form of the verb *to be*. An adjective may follow other state-of-being verbs.

Some Forms of *Be*	Some Other State-of-Being Verbs
am is was has been should have been	looks feels seems appears becomes

Notice the bold adjectives after the verbs in these example sentences.

EXAMPLES   The winner was **surprised**. She looked **shocked**.

"I am **amazed** and **speechless**," she said.

Activity B   Complete each sentence with an adjective. Write the adjective on your paper.

1) The trees were _____.

2) My English teacher seems _____.

3) Movies about romance are _____.

4) I would like to drive a car that is _____.

5) Tests can be _____.

Activity C   Add adjectives to each sentence. Write new sentences.

1) The _____ girl did a _____ somersault.

2) Did you order _____ jam on _____ toast?

3) After running _____ miles, Derek said, "I feel _____ and _____!"

4) The _____ dessert made everyone feel _____.

5) The United States is a _____ and _____ country.

6) School subjects that are _____ can also be _____.

Exact Adjectives

You can help your readers to form sharp pictures. Use exact adjectives. Avoid general, vague adjectives such as *good, nice, bad,* and *pretty.* Try to be exact instead.

EXAMPLES	Vague:	It was a *nice* morning.
	Sharper:	It was a *sunny, breezy* morning.
	Vague:	The pizza tasted *good.*
	Sharper:	The pizza tasted *spicy* and *hot.*
	Vague:	Mia painted a *pretty* picture.
	Sharper:	Mia painted a *colorful* picture.

Thesaurus

A reference source that lists words and their synonyms.

When you are trying to come up with an exact adjective, a **thesaurus** can help. A thesaurus is a book that lists words with similar meanings, or **synonyms.** You can also find a thesaurus in some word-processing software programs.

Use a thesaurus to choose the synonym that fits best with your meaning. Look at the examples below.

Synonyms

Words that have a similar meaning. (big and large; happy and glad)

Vague Adjectives	Sharper Synonyms
a *bad* storm	furious, dangerous, threatening, powerful
a *bad* dog	mischievous, disobedient, stubborn, vicious
a *bad* taste	sickening, stale, bitter, rotten

Activity D   Each bold adjective below is not as sharp as it could be. Replace the adjective with a sharper one. Use a thesaurus if you wish. Write the new sentence on your paper.

1) My best friend is **nice.**

2) The sky looks **nice.**

3) Write a **good** sentence.

4) The team had a **bad** game.

5) Those flowers are **pretty.**

Adverbs

An **adverb** is another kind of describing word. Adverbs often give details about actions. Each bold adverb below modifies a verb. Notice the question that each adverb answers.

EXAMPLES

When?
Today we'll shop **early** and eat **later**.

How?
Read **slowly** and **carefully**. Write **clearly**.

How often?
Wages are paid **weekly**. Check in **daily**.

Where?
Put your coat **there**. We'll go **outside**.

Each adverb below modifies an adjective or another adverb. Such adverbs tell about intensity or degree.

EXAMPLE

To what degree?
The girls were **extremely** worried. Benjy ran **too** quickly. He was **almost** lost.

The adverbs of degree include *very* and *quite*, which can be overused. When you check your writing, see whether you have used *very* or *quite* too often. You may be able to cross out these overused words without changing your meaning.

Activity E Read the sentences below. Decide what question is answered by each bold adverb. Write the question on your paper. Here are the questions to choose from: *When? How? How often? Where? To what degree?*

1) **Immediately**, the door slammed shut.
2) The bell rings **hourly**.
3) Everyone is **very** busy.
4) The baby smiled **happily**.
5) We looked **everywhere** for the keys.
6) The weather **suddenly** turned cold.
7) Derek will run **tomorrow**.

Adjective or Adverb?

You have probably noticed that many adverbs end in -*ly*. You can often change an adjective into an adverb by adding -*ly*. If the adjective ends in -*y*, change the *y* to *i* before adding -*ly*.

EXAMPLES	**Adjective**	**Adverb**
	Amanda is **careful**.	Amanda works **carefully**.
	We feel **happy**.	We smiled **happily**.
	He gave an **angry** stare.	He stared **angrily**.

Activity F Change the adjective in parentheses into an adverb. Write the completed sentence on your paper.

1) The boy yawned (sleepy).
2) The dog guarded the house (brave).
3) The woman in the painting smiles (mysterious).
4) My aunt sings (beautiful).
5) "Ho, ho, ho!" the man laughed (merry).

Try to avoid making mistakes with adjectives and adverbs. One common mistake is using an adjective when an adverb is needed. Remember that an adjective cannot modify an action verb. Only an adverb modifies an action verb.

EXAMPLES	Incorrect:	He spoke too **rapid**.
	Correct:	He spoke too **rapidly**.
	Incorrect:	The dancer moves **graceful**.
	Correct:	The dancer moves **gracefully**.

Activity G Choose the word in parentheses that correctly completes the sentence. Write the completed sentence on your paper.

1) The sky at sunset is so (colorful, colorfully).
2) Try to spell all words (correct, correctly).
3) The fielder caught the ball (easy, easily).
4) We sat here (peaceful, peacefully).
5) "My head feels (dizzy, dizzily)," said Mia.

Placement of Adverbs

Notice the bold adverb in these three sentences:

 Adverbs **often** move.

Often, adverbs move.

Adverbs move **often**.

To add variety to your sentences, try moving your adverbs around. If you decide to place an adverb first in a sentence, add a comma after it to show a pause.

Activity H   Find the adverb in each sentence below. Then rewrite the sentence. Change the placement of the adverb. If you use the adverb as the first word in the sentence, you may need to add a comma.

The Tennis Tournament
by Mike Kaplan

1) I bravely entered the tennis tournament in my neighborhood.

2) I actually thought I might win.

3) These thoughts of grandeur occasionally enter my head.

4) I faced my opponent calmly.

5) My serve has been strong lately.

6) I soon saw that the other player was experienced.

7) "I will certainly win at least a few games," I told myself.

8) I won a few points accidentally.

9) The match was over rapidly.

10) My friends immediately congratulated me for trying.

Comparisons

You can make comparisons using adjectives and adverbs. Each adjective and adverb has three forms: **positive, comparative,** and **superlative.**

1. Use the comparative form when you are comparing just two people, places, things, or actions. Use the comparative form whenever your comparison includes the word *than.*

EXAMPLES	Positive	Comparative
	Luis is **tall** and **thin**.	Luis is **taller** and **thinner** than his father.
	He walks **quickly**.	He walks **more quickly** than most people.

2. Use the superlative form when you are comparing more than two people, places, things, or actions.

EXAMPLES	Positive	Superlative
	Laura sang **beautifully**.	Of all the singers, Laura sang **most beautifully**.
	She is **talented**.	She is the **most talented** music student in the class.

3. For most one-syllable words and some two-syllable words, add the ending *-er* to form the comparative. Add *-est* to form the superlative.

EXAMPLES	Positive	Comparative	Superlative
	tall	taller	tallest
	thin	thinner	thinnest
	young	younger	youngest
	wise	wiser	wisest
	fast	faster	fastest
	big	bigger	biggest
	happy	happier	happiest

4. With words of more than one syllable, use *more* and *most* to form the comparative and superlative forms.

EXAMPLES	Positive	Comparative	Superlative
	beautiful	more beautiful	most beautiful
	bravely	more bravely	most bravely
	sudden	more sudden	most sudden
	expensive	more expensive	most expensive
	sensible	more sensible	most sensible
	careful	more careful	most careful

Activity I Copy the following chart on your paper. Fill in the missing positive, comparative, and superlative forms of the words.

	Positive	Comparative	Superlative
1)	big	bigger	_____
2)	slow	_____	slowest
3)	_____	older	oldest
4)	happy	_____	happiest
5)	happily	more happily	_____
6)	ugly	_____	ugliest
7)	bravely	more bravely	_____
8)	lazy	lazier	_____
9)	expensive	_____	most expensive
10)	_____	whiter	whitest
11)	graceful	_____	most graceful
12)	_____	louder	loudest

5. Use *less* for the comparative form and *least* for the superlative form with all adjectives and adverbs.

EXAMPLES	Positive	Comparative	Superlative
	new	less new	least new
	expensive	less expensive	least expensive
	often	less often	least often
	civilized	less civilized	least civilized

Activity J Read each sentence. The positive form of the adjective or adverb is in parentheses. Decide whether the positive, comparative, or superlative form belongs in the sentence. Write the form on your paper.

1) What is the (beautiful) park in the United States?

2) When you are ill, you feel (lively) than usual.

3) A turtle moves (fast) than a snail.

4) Of these ten words, which one do you (often) misspell?

5) Laura is a (strong) person.

6) Cookies are (fattening) than fruit.

7) Celery is probably the (fattening) of any food.

8) This maple tree is (big) than that one.

9) Which of these two trees is (large)?

10) "Running is (easy) than tennis," said Derek.

11) Max was the (small) puppy in the litter.

12) Tell me the (interesting) thing you heard.

Comparing Correctly

A few adjectives and adverbs have irregular comparative and superlative forms. Study the list below.

Positive	Comparative	Superlative
good, well	better	best
bad, badly	worse	worst
many, much	more	most
little	less	least

Make sure that you use only the forms above when you compare with these adjectives and adverbs.

EXAMPLES   Incorrect: Today I feel even worser than yesterday.

Correct: Today I feel even worse than yesterday.

Activity K   Read each sentence below. Write the word that correctly completes the sentence.

1) I have read three books by Tony Hillerman, and I liked *A Thief of Time* (well, better, best).

2) That was the (bad, worse, worst) movie ever made!

3) Ahmed played very (well, better, best) in the chess tournament.

4) (Little, Less, Least) rain fell this month than last month.

5) (Much, More, Most) rain falls in July than in December.

Study this final rule for comparing correctly.

6. Avoid double comparisons. Use either the ending -er or the word *more*—not both. Use either the ending -est or the word *most*—not both. Do not add endings if you are comparing with *less* or *least*.

EXAMPLES	Incorrect:	This room is the most cleanest it's ever been!
	Correct:	This room is the cleanest it's ever been!
	Incorrect:	Which car is less noisier?
	Correct:	Which car is less noisy?

Activity L   Find the error in each sentence. Rewrite the sentence correctly.

1) Today's lunch was more gooder than yesterday's.

2) Summer is the most laziest time of the year.

3) Which of these two brands is more cheaper?

4) The more worsest storm of the year hit the coast.

5) Stores hire more people during the most busiest shopping season.

6) Today is the least busiest day of the week.

7) Your painting is more better than mine.

8) Which train arrives more sooner?

9) The friends met less oftener.

10) We chose the most best day for the party.

Adjectives and adverbs are words that describe. Make your sentences clearer and more interesting by adding adjectives and adverbs.

- Use exact adjectives instead of vague ones.
- Use an adverb to modify an action verb.
- Move adverbs to give your sentences variety.
- Use the positive, comparative, and superlative forms correctly.

Part A   These sentences are not as sharp and clear as they could be. Rewrite each sentence. You may change a vague adjective into an exact adjective. You may add adjectives and adverbs. You may also change the word order. Use a thesaurus if you wish.

1) Amanda always looks very nice.
2) Ocean water often feels quite good.
3) I would like to buy a good recording.
4) The weather is bad today.
5) This TV program is usually pretty good.

Part B   Find one error in each sentence below. Rewrite the sentence correctly.

1) Mike's serve is more better than Derek's.
2) Laura can sing highly or low.
3) "Look at what I did," the child said proud.
4) Amanda has several sweaters, but she wears her blue one more often.
5) Victor baked bread careful.
6) Victor's bread smells extremely freshly.
7) Does Computer Village have the most lowest prices?
8) Which of these two computers is least expensive?
9) Ming is older than Mia, but Mia is tallest.
10) "I've just had the horriblest day of my life," announced Yasmin wearily.

Phrase

A group of words that does not contain a subject or predicate, such as a prepositional phrase or a verb phrase.

A group of words in a sentence is sometimes called a **phrase**. Add phrases to your sentences to make your information clearer. A **prepositional phrase** works like an adjective or an adverb in a sentence.

A prepositional phrase begins with a word called a preposition. A preposition shows a connection between a noun or a pronoun and another word. A preposition often shows direction. Some common prepositions are listed below.

Prepositional phrase

A group of words made up of a preposition and its object; it may be used as either an adjective or an adverb (to the store, by the road).

Prepositions		
about	between	near
across	beyond	of
after	by	on
against	during	out
among	for	over
around	from	to
at	in	under
behind	into	with

A prepositional phrase ends with a word called the object. The object of the preposition is a noun or a pronoun. Study these examples.

EXAMPLES		
Preposition	**Object**	**Prepositional Phrase Used in a Sentence**
to	school	He walked to school.
for	him	We bought a present for him.
with	me	Come with me.
from	Karen	I answered the phone call from Karen.

Other words may come between the preposition and the object in a prepositional phrase. A sentence may include more than one prepositional phrase. Read the example sentences below. Notice how the bold prepositional phrases add information to the sentence. The preposition that begins each phrase is underlined.

> **EXAMPLES**   We jumped **into the extremely cold water of the lake**.
>
> A message **from my friend in Denver** appeared **on my computer screen**.

Activity A   Find twenty-five prepositional phrases in these sentences. List them on your paper.

1) The girl in the middle of that photo is my sister.

2) Look for prepositional phrases in this sentence.

3) Benjy hid his bone under the tree in the yard.

4) Derek works at the garage several days a week.

5) The children stared at the storyteller as he told a tale of mystery.

6) For several months, snow covers most of the land.

7) One of the students in the class is absent.

8) The house on the hill belongs to my grandmother.

9) Which of these plays is by Shakespeare?

10) The desk by the window is broken.

11) Stella sat behind Luis during the concert.

12) What begins with a preposition and has an object at the end?

13) Sonia left a message for Vincent on his answering machine.

14) He called her after work.

Adjective Phrases

A prepositional phrase may do the job of an adjective. It modifies a noun or pronoun in a sentence. Compare the adjective and the adjective phrase in these examples.

EXAMPLES   Adjective: The **middle** girl is my sister.

                    Adjective phrase: The girl **in the middle** is my sister.

Activity B   Each sentence contains a prepositional phrase used as an adjective. Write each bold adjective phrase on your paper. Write the word that the adjective phrase describes.

Example   The book **about kangaroos** was missing.
about kangaroos — book.

1) We read a poem **by Edgar Allan Poe**.

2) The letter **from Karen** was short.

3) How often is the rodeo **in Centerville** held?

4) A house **near a highway** can be noisy.

5) Would you like ice cream **with peaches**?

Activity C   Rewrite the sentences below. Add a prepositional phrase after each bold noun. The new phrase must describe that noun.

Example   That **woman** is my aunt.
That woman in the red dress is my aunt.

1) George Washington was the first **president**.

2) The **capital** is Indianapolis.

3) The **man** won the race.

4) The **building** is ten stories high.

5) Amanda received a birthday **card**.

Adverb Phrases

A prepositional phrase may do the job of an adverb. It modifies a verb, an adjective, or another adverb. Compare the adverb and the adverb phrase in these examples. The adverb and the phrase both answer the same question.

EXAMPLES		
Adverb:	Sit **nearby**. (sit *where?*)	
Adverb phrase:	Sit **near me**. (sit *where?*)	
Adverb:	He arrived **later**. (arrived *when?*)	
Adverb phrase:	He arrived **in the evening**. (arrived *when?*)	
Adverb:	Please drive **carefully**. (drive *how?*)	
Adverb phrase:	Please drive **with care**. (drive *how?*)	
Adverb:	We are **truly** sorry. (sorry *to what degree?*)	
Adverb phrase:	We are sorry **beyond measure**. (sorry *to what degree?*)	

Activity D Each sentence contains a prepositional phrase used as an adverb. Write each bold verb on your paper. Write the adverb phrase that modifies the verb.

Example The friends **walked** to the store.
walked — to the store.

1) We **read** the poem by ourselves.

2) Columbus **reached** the island in 1492.

3) The girls **drove** to Centerville.

4) The dog **walked** with a limp.

5) He **arrived** by plane.

Activity E Use each adverb phrase in a sentence. Make sure that the phrase modifies a verb.

1) across the road

2) by a few inches

3) at the store

4) behind a tree

5) with the principal

6) on time

7) into the pot

8) against my will

9) between four and five o'clock

10) during lunch

Placement of Prepositional Phrases

Think about where you place prepositional phrases in your sentences. In general, place an adjective phrase close to the word it modifies. An adverb phrase, like an adverb, can move around in a sentence. Vary your sentences by putting adverb phrases in different positions. Here are examples of correctly placed adverb phrases.

> **EXAMPLES**
>
> Amanda went to her locker **between classes**.
> **Between classes**, Amanda went to her locker.
>
> What do you like to do **in your spare time**?
> **In your spare time**, what do you like to do?

Make sure that the phrase is not placed where it may confuse readers.

> **EXAMPLES**
>
> Unclear: We learned how to use sunlight to start a fire **in our science class**.
>
> Clear: **In our science class**, we learned how to use sunlight to start a fire.

Activity F Find the prepositional phrase in each sentence below. If the sentence is clear, copy the sentence. If the prepositional phrase should be moved, rewrite the sentence correctly.

1) The smells are wonderful in Grandmother's kitchen.

2) The dog guarded the house for three days.

3) The friends talked about the party in the hallway.

4) The audience left the theater after the first act.

5) The apartment has a big hall closet with two bedrooms.

6) A doctor may advise a patient to get more exercise during a physical exam.

7) A woman spoke to our class from Sweden.

Activity G   Look again at the sentences you wrote for Activity F. Rewrite three of the sentences by putting the prepositional phrase in a different position. Make sure that the sentence is still clear.

Between or Among

Careful writers know how to choose between the prepositions *between* and *among*. Each word has a different use.

- Use *between* when you are discussing two people or things.

- Use *among* when you are discussing three or more people or things.

EXAMPLES	Can you see Laura among all those students?
	Laura is sitting between Mike and Amanda.

Activity H   Write *between* or *among* to complete each sentence correctly.

1) When Derek is (between, among) his friends, he is not shy.

2) The members of the group divided the work (between, among) themselves.

3) Some students eat lunch (between, among) third and fourth periods.

4) "Let's split the money (between, among) us," Roy told Arnold.

5) (Between, Among) the two of them, they managed to get the work done.

Improve your sentences by adding prepositional phrases.

- Use an adjective phrase to describe a noun or a pronoun.
- Use an adverb phrase to describe a verb, an adjective, or an adverb.

Part A Find ten prepositional phrases in these sentences. List them in order on your paper. Label each one *adjective phrase* or *adverb phrase*.

1) Amanda bought a thesaurus at a store in Springfield.

2) A thesaurus has lists of words.

3) The words are listed by meanings.

4) Words with similar meanings are synonyms.

5) A thesaurus may list words with opposite meanings, too.

6) The name of an opposite word is *antonym*.

7) Amanda brings her thesaurus with her to English class.

8) During this year, Amanda has improved her vocabulary.

Part B Write five sentences using all of the prepositional phrases below.

at the end	of the road
with a big smile	for a friend
from Chicago	in the front row
between two classes	during the morning

Show your readers how your ideas are connected. Combine sentences that have related ideas. By combining sentences, you can also avoid short, choppy sentences.

Read the first paragraph below. Notice how it seems to go on forever! The one sentence below it combines all the ideas simply.

EXAMPLE	Not combined:	Amanda is Laura's friend. Mike is Derek's friend. Derek is Amanda's friend. Amanda is Mike's friend. Laura is Mike's friend. Derek is Laura's friend.
	Combined:	Amanda, Laura, Derek, and Mike are all friends.

The word *and* is an example of a conjunction. Conjunctions are used to show connections among ideas in sentences. Other examples of conjunctions are *but, or, yet,* and *so.*

Activity A   Read each pair of sentences. Add the conjunction in parentheses, and combine the sentences. Write each sentence on your paper. Remember to put a comma before the conjunction.

Example   Is this statement true? Is it false? (or)
            Is this statement true, or is it false?

1) Some sentences can be short. Others can be long. (and)

2) Marcella likes Ahmed. He has never noticed her. (but)

3) You may choose a short story. You may prefer a novel. (or)

4) Mr. Johnson became rich. He never forgot his poor childhood. (yet)

5) Laura was going to have a Spanish test on Monday. She studied all weekend. (so)

Using the Conjunction *and*

Use the conjunction *and* to connect words, phrases, and sentences. Study the examples below to see how the conjunction improves sentences.

EXAMPLES		
Choppy:	We planted tomatoes.
	We planted cabbage.
	We planted peppers.
Connected words:	We planted tomatoes, cabbage, **and** peppers.
Choppy:	She looked under the bed.
	She looked in the closet.
Connected phrases:	She looked under the bed **and** in the closet.
Not connected clearly:	Write a good sentence. The world is yours!
Combined sentences:	Write a good sentence, **and** the world is yours!

Study these two rules for using commas with the conjunction *and*.

1. Use a comma to separate a series of three or more words or phrases. Put a comma before the conjunction *and*. If only one item comes before the *and*, do not use a comma.

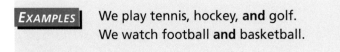

> **EXAMPLES**   We play tennis, hockey, **and** golf.
> We watch football **and** basketball.

2. Use a comma before the conjunction when you combine two or more sentences.

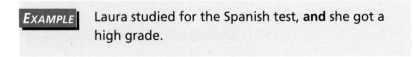

> **EXAMPLE**   Laura studied for the Spanish test, **and** she got a high grade.

Activity B Combine each set of three choppy sentences. Use the conjunction *and*. Write each combined sentence on your paper.

1) Monday it rained. Tuesday it rained. Wednesday it rained.

2) I like swimming. I like cooking. I like listening to music.

3) The dog was lost. The dog was tired. The dog was hungry.

4) Charles is late. Rhonda is late. Their daughter is late.

5) We marched up the hill. We marched down the hill. We marched across a field.

Activity C Each sentence has at least one error. Rewrite the sentence correctly.

1) Springfield is a large town and it is growing rapidly.

2) Victor signed up for classes in baking breads, and pies.

3) Jean-Claude speaks English, French and, Creole.

4) Mr. Martin teaches at the high school, and lives a few blocks away.

5) The rodeo events include calf roping bareback riding and barrel racing.

6) Mr. Johnson loves to read and he owns many books.

7) The children swam in the ocean, and played on the beach.

8) Anita plays basketball soccer, and tennis.

9) Chicago New York and Los Angeles are all big cities.

10) The dancers leaped whirled and stepped gracefully.

Using the Conjunction *but*

You have seen that the conjunction *and* connects related ideas. Use the conjunction *but* to point out a difference between ideas. A difference is also called a contrast. Notice the contrasts in the examples on the next page.

EXAMPLES	Related ideas:	I like tea **and** coffee.
	Contrasting ideas:	I like tea **but** not coffee.
	Related ideas:	I enjoy pets, **and** I have two cats.
	Contrasting ideas:	I enjoy pets, **but** I am allergic to them.

Activity D   Decide whether each of the following sentences contains related ideas or contrasting ideas. Write each sentence on your paper. Use *and* or *but* to complete each sentence correctly.

1) Amanda has a dog, (and, but) Laura does not.

2) Both Amanda (and, but) Laura are friends of Derek's.

3) Amanda wanted to go to dancing class, (and, but) it was canceled.

4) Laura sings in the chorus, (and, but) she did not sing tonight.

5) Springfield has city parks (and, but) golf courses.

6) Mike likes to play tennis, (and, but) he is usually at the courts early Saturday morning.

7) The family enjoys hiking, camping, (and, but) fishing.

8) A dictionary is one useful source for writers, (and, but) a thesaurus is another.

9) Most deserts are hot, (and, but) some are cold.

10) The island has birds and lizards (and, but) no mammals.

11) The drivers honked their horns, (and, but) the traffic did not move.

12) Most snakes do not harm people, (and, but) many people fear snakes anyway.

Other Conjunctions

You have seen how the conjunctions *and* and *but* are used to connect ideas in sentences. You may also use the conjunctions *or, so,* and *yet* to connect ideas. Read the example sentences below. Notice how the bold conjunctions connect words, phrases, or **independent clauses**.

Independent clause
A group of words that includes a subject and a verb. It may be written alone as a complete sentence, or it may be combined with another clause.

EXAMPLES	I like coffee **or** tea.
	Will he travel by car, **or** will he take the bus?
	He said he would come by car, **yet** he arrived by bus.
	The woman was old **yet** looked young.
	The show had begun, **so** everyone hurried.

Look for the commas in the example sentences above. You should see that they follow this rule:

- When you join two independent clauses with the conjunction *and, but, or, yet,* or *so,* use a comma before the conjunction.

Some conjunctions work in pairs: *either...or, neither...nor, not only...but also.* Notice the bold paired conjunctions below.

EXAMPLES	You may choose to read **either** a poem **or** a story.
	Neither Amanda **nor** Mike has arrived.
	The dog was **not only** lost **but also** wet and muddy.

Activity E
List the conjunctions you find in each of the following sentences.

1) The class will read a short story or several poems.

2) It was August, yet the weather grew cold.

3) The winds blew not only from the east but also from the north.

4) I will either phone you tonight or see you tomorrow.

5) The dog had hidden the keys, so Ms. O'Hara never found them.

6) Neither the son nor the daughter looks like the mother.

Activity F Think of words that could complete each sentence below. Write the completed sentence on your paper.

1) Either the doorbell rang, or

2) The sun is shining, and

3) The room seemed empty, yet

4) We have neither the time nor

5) I thought I knew the answer, but

Activity G Combine each pair of sentences. Use one of the conjunctions from the box. Rewrite each sentence on your paper. Use commas correctly. (These sentences can be combined in more than one way.)

| or | yet | so | and | but | either/or |

1) Yesterday it was cold. It was rainy.

2) Would you like tea? Would you like coffee?

3) We planted peas in our garden. They did not come up.

4) The party was boring. We left early.

5) The runner came in third. She seemed pleased.

6) You may do your homework before dinner. You may do it after dinner.

Subordinating Conjunctions

Subordinating conjunction

A conjunction that joins a dependent clause to an independent clause (because, when, since).

Some conjunctions do not connect independent clauses. A conjunction such as *because, although, when, since,* or *until* is called a **subordinating conjunction**. A subordinating conjunction is the first word of a **dependent clause**. A dependent clause cannot stand alone because it is not a complete idea.

Dependent clause

A group of related words that contains a subject and a verb but that does not express a complete idea (Before the phone rang).

Notice the bold dependent clause in each sentence below. Notice that it begins with an underlined subordinating conjunction.

EXAMPLES The boys played tennis **until it got dark**.

When the car stopped working, we took it to the garage.

When you use a subordinating conjunction, make sure that you have an independent clause in the sentence. If there is only a dependent clause, you have written a sentence fragment.

Activity H Label each group of words below as *Sentence* or *Fragment*. If it is a fragment, turn it into a complete sentence.

1) Although Ahmed likes to win at chess.

2) Since it was late.

3) Because the sun was shining brightly.

4) When Laura sings, everyone listens.

5) Because the United States was once a British colony.

6) Although Bo is small, he is very strong.

7) Until the movie ended.

8) When the fire began, no one was home.

Follow these two rules for using commas with subordinating conjunctions.

1. If the sentence begins with a dependent clause, put a comma after the clause.

| EXAMPLE | **When we arrived,** the game had already begun. |

2. Do not use a comma if the dependent clause comes after the independent clause.

| EXAMPLE | The game had already begun **when we arrived**. |

Activity I Write each of these subordinating conjunctions in a sentence. In four of the sentences, make the conjunction the first word of the sentence. Check to see that you have used commas correctly.

1) after

5) unless

2) although

6) until

3) because

7) when

4) if

8) whenever

Activity J Read the paragraph below. Combine sentences by using these subordinating conjunctions: *when, because, although, until, if.* Write the paragraph in eight sentences. Check to be sure you have punctuated each sentence correctly.

Never Give Up!
by Mike Kaplan

I lost my first tennis match. I was not playing well. I expected to improve. I needed to practice every day. My friend Derek practiced with me. He gave me good pointers. The first defeat had been maddening. I entered another tournament. I played my best. I won the first match! I continued to play well. I lost in the second round. I definitely had improved. The scores were only 6–2 and 6–4. I plan to keep on trying.

You can combine ideas to make your sentences clear and varied. Use conjunctions to combine ideas.

- Use *and* to combine related ideas. Use *but* to show a contrast.
- Use conjunctions to combine words, phrases, or independent clauses. Use commas when needed.
- Use a subordinating conjunction to connect a dependent clause to an independent clause. If the dependent clause comes first, use a comma to separate it from the rest of the sentence.

Lesson Review   Read the following sentences. Pay attention to the conjunctions and punctuation. Find the mistakes. Rewrite the sentences to show ten correct sentences.

1) I planned to relax last evening but we had visitors.

2) Not only my sister and also her husband and baby came to visit.

3) Tamara Rick and, Michelle stayed for hours.

4) Although my mother was happy to see them. I cannot say that I was.

5) Babies have always seemed noisy, and boring to me.

6) They are always either crying. Or sleeping.

7) Michelle gave me a big smile, whenever she looked at me.

8) She is just one year old. Yet she says lots of words.

9) She not only says "Derek" but she also says "Uncle."

10) Michelle seems smarter than other babies. Because she is my niece.

Part A   Rewrite these sentences. Change each bold word into a sharper adjective. Then add one more adjective to the sentence.

Examples   Today is **nice**.
Today is warm and sunny.

1) The friends watched a **good** movie.
2) The lake is a **nice** place to visit.
3) The bread smells **great**.
4) Your sweater is **pretty**.
5) A **bad** storm hit the town.

Part B   Answer each question by adding an adverb or a prepositional phrase to the sentence. Write the new sentence.

1) The weather is hot. (When?)
2) The dog barked. (How?)
3) We will go on a trip. (Where?)
4) We will go on a trip. (How?)
5) Arnold arrived late. (To what degree?)

Part C   Choose the modifier in parentheses that correctly completes the sentence. Write the completed sentence on your paper.

1) The water is (less calm, least calm, less calmer) today than yesterday.
2) "That is the (worstest, most worse, worst) music I've ever heard!" said Mr. Noyes.
3) Tessa chose the (redder, reddest, more redder) shoes she could find.
4) Does Brand X get sheets (whiter, more whiter, most white) than Brand Y?
5) The bear growled (angrily, angry, angriest).

Part D   Use each of these modifiers correctly in a sentence.

1) highly	**6)** daily
2) sometimes	**7)** usually
3) harmful	**8)** better
4) gently	**9)** worse
5) gentlest	**10)** more quietly

Part E   Combine the ideas in the sentences below. Use a conjunction. Write the new sentence.

1) Derek would like to be a mechanic. He knows he will work hard.

2) Laura has a clear voice. She has a beautiful voice.

3) Mike plays tennis. He is improving his game.

4) Amanda has known Mike for years. She has never met his brother.

5) Mr. Johnson does not watch TV. He does not go to movies.

6) Is Ahmed playing chess? Is he watching a game?

7) Jean-Claude speaks Creole. His family comes from Haiti.

8) They tried to play soccer. It rained.

9) Basketball is a fast game. Hockey is even faster.

10) Get the necessary ingredients and cooking utensils. Cook your favorite meal.

Test Taking Tip   When you have vocabulary to learn, make flash cards. Write a word on the front of each card. Write the definition on the back. Use the flash cards in a game to test your vocabulary skills.

Chapter 7

The Parts of a Paragraph

Picture a page of print from a magazine, a newspaper, or any book. Now imagine that the print is NOT broken into separate blocks of type. All the sentences run together. That page would seem hard to read, wouldn't it?

Blocks of type, or paragraphs, make a page easier to read. Paragraphs also have the important job of showing readers how ideas are organized. Do you know how to break your writing into paragraphs? Do you know how to use paragraphs to help your readers follow your ideas?

In this chapter, you will learn how to build a clearly organized paragraph.

Goals for Learning

▶ To write a topic sentence that prepares the reader for the main idea of a paragraph

▶ To write sentences that develop the main idea of a paragraph

▶ To end a paragraph with a conclusion or a summary statement

Paragraph

A group of sentences about one idea or topic. It usually has three parts: a topic sentence or introduction, a body, and a conclusion or summary.

A **paragraph** is a group of sentences about one idea or topic. The first sentence of each paragraph is indented on a new line. When you write a new paragraph, your readers expect to find a new idea. You can help them by writing a **topic sentence**. It tells what the paragraph is going to be about.

Since you are the writer of the paragraph, only you know what its main idea should be. Think before writing the first sentence. Here are some questions to ask yourself:

1. What is the purpose of this paragraph?

Topic sentence

A sentence that states the main idea in a paragraph; it is often the first sentence.

2. What is the main point I want to make?

3. Why am I writing this paragraph?

4. What will this paragraph be about?

Read the paragraph below. Think about how the bold topic sentence prepares the reader for the main idea.

Adjectives can be words of power. Writers try to choose exact adjectives that express meaning sharply and clearly. Careful writers avoid adjectives such as *nice* and *bad*, which have little meaning. The best adjective is one that paints a clear picture. An adjective with a specific meaning is a word of power.

Activity A   Reread the paragraph about adjectives. Write another topic sentence for it that states the main idea.

Activity B   Read the four facts below. Write a topic sentence for these facts. Your topic sentence should state the main idea for a paragraph that includes these facts.

Fact 1:   Walt Disney was a film producer.

Fact 2:   He produced famous movies, including *Mary Poppins* and *Treasure Island*.

Fact 3:   Many of his films were cartoons, such as *Cinderella*, *Fantasia*, and *Pinocchio*.

Fact 4:   The Disney Studio won forty-five Oscars during Walt Disney's lifetime.

A topic sentence is a general statement. Examples and details are in the rest of the paragraph. Read the sample paragraph below. The first sentence is the topic sentence. Do you see how it introduces the topic in a general way?

> Springfield is a pleasant place to live. The weather is comfortably warm most of the year. The town has many parks, stores, museums, and restaurants. The townspeople are known for their friendly and helpful attitude. Springfield citizens are proud of their town.

Activity C Read each set of sentences below. Decide which one would work best as the topic sentence of a paragraph. Write the letter of your answer.

1) a) Car owners must check their oil.

   b) Car owners must check the air pressure in the tires.

   c) Car owners need to do regular checks.

2) a) A topic sentence has two main jobs.

   b) A topic sentence expresses a main idea.

   c) A topic sentence prepares readers for a new idea.

3) a) Some students go to college right after high school.

   b) Students have decisions to make.

   c) Some students choose to work after graduation.

Activity D Read the following paragraph. It has no topic sentence. Write a sentence that expresses the main idea of this paragraph.

> A tennis player needs a good forehand. A forehand is used when the ball comes to a right-handed player's right side. The player also needs a backhand. A backhand is used when the ball comes to the player's left side. These two strokes are the ones that a tennis player uses most often.

To write a topic sentence, you must start with an idea. Where do ideas for paragraphs come from? Here are some answers:

- Your own experiences
- Reading what others have written
- Information you have received from people

Ideas come from everywhere and from everything that you experience and imagine. Read the examples of topics below. Look at how each topic suggests a topic sentence.

EXAMPLES	Examples of Topics	Possible Topic Sentences
	The fire department	Our local fire department helps the community in many ways.
	Camping	Before you go camping, you will need some equipment.
	Chess	Each of the six chess pieces moves in a different way.

Activity E Practice writing topic sentences. Make a list of five topics on your paper. Choose from the list below, or use topics of your own.

- Sports or other athletic activities
- People
- Hobbies
- Places
- Books, movies, or television programs
- Organizations or clubs

Write a topic sentence about each of your five topics. The examples above can guide you.

Titles and Topic Sentences

The title of a paragraph is like a topic sentence in one way. Both express the main idea. A title and a topic sentence, however, are different. A title is usually a phrase and not a complete sentence. The topic sentence tells the reader more about the topic than the title does.

Compare the title and the topic sentences below. The title only names the topic. A topic sentence sets the tone for the rest of the paragraph. Study the examples below to see the difference between a title and a topic sentence. Do you see how topic sentences 1 and 2 will lead to very different paragraphs?

EXAMPLES	Title of Paragraph:	Roller Coasters
	Topic Sentence 1:	A ride on a roller coaster is a thrilling, fascinating, speeding moment in time.
	Topic Sentence 2:	The very word *roller coaster* creates an unforgettable picture in my mind—a picture of sheer terror.

Activity F   Read the paragraph titles below. Write a topic sentence that could prepare the reader for a paragraph with that title.

1) Walt Disney: A Hollywood Genius

2) Why I Enjoy My Garden

3) Five Reasons for Owning a Computer

4) My Future as a Millionaire

5) Beginning a Paragraph

Begin a paragraph with a topic sentence. Your topic sentence should state the main idea of your paragraph.

Part A Write a topic sentence on your paper for each set of details below.

1) Car owners should change their oil.
   They should check the hoses for leaks.
   They should also check the air pressure in the tires regularly.

2) Books are excellent sources of information.
   Books can also be read purely for fun.
   People have written thousands of books on every topic you can imagine.

3) First, set the oven temperature.
   Next, gather all the ingredients.
   Finally, follow the steps on the recipe.

4) The wind blew down several trees.
   The electricity was out for two hours.
   The streets were flooded.

5) We packed a big lunch.
   We also took baseball bats, balls, and gloves.
   We took several lawn chairs, too.

Part B Read the following titles. Write a topic sentence about each title.

1) My Favorite Movie

2) Music I Like

3) If I Were a Millionaire

4) My Family

5) The Way I Feel Today

Body

The part of a paragraph that discusses the main idea; these sentences can include reasons, facts, examples, or illustrations.

What do you do after you have stated your main idea in a topic sentence? Your next job is to develop that main idea. The sentences that tell more about the main idea make up the **body** of a paragraph. Think of the body as a few sentences that support the idea stated in the topic sentence. In the body, you make the main idea clearer to your reader.

Include any of these elements in the body of your paragraph:

- Facts
- Details
- Explanations
- Reasons
- Examples
- Illustrations

Activity A   Practice developing a main idea. Copy the topic sentence shown below on your paper. Then use the details that follow to write three sentences. All of the sentences must be about the main idea stated in the topic sentence.

Topic Sentence: Springfield is a town with many places for recreation.

Recreational Places in Springfield

- 4 city parks
- a sports arena
- a concert hall
- 3 recreational centers
- 2 public swimming pools
- 2 golf courses
- 9 public tennis courts
- a museum
- an amusement park
- 5 movie theaters

Activity B   Read the following topic sentences. Choose the topic that you know the most about. Write at least three sentences that support the topic sentence.

- Everyone needs a hobby.
- Americans are fortunate people.
- Someday, I plan to be a great success in the field of (name of occupation).

Sticking to the Topic

The sentences in the body of a paragraph support the main idea. Sometimes, you may find one or two sentences that are off the topic. Take those sentences out of your paragraph, or rewrite them so that they fit better with the topic.

Read the following paragraph. Look for one sentence that is off the topic.

> Summer is the best time of year for vacations. Children do not have to go to school. Freedom from classes allows time for sleeping late on sunny mornings. Usually the pleasant weather is suitable for outdoor hobbies: tennis, running, gardening, or just lying lazily in the yard. Sometimes, spring is also a good time for a vacation. In summer, the beaches and the mountains have many activities for tourists. Vacationers can surf or swim, hike or explore, for hours on end. It is no wonder that vacation spots do big business in summer.

Did you find the sentence that was off the topic? All the sentences support the main idea that summer is the best time for vacations. Only one sentence tells about a different topic: *Sometimes, spring is also a good time for a vacation.* That sentence about springtime vacations belongs in a different paragraph.

Activity C   Read each paragraph below and at the top of the next page. Copy the one sentence that does not belong in the body of each paragraph. Write a sentence on your paper that tells why it does not belong.

1) > Edgar Allan Poe is famous for his bizarre short stories. One of his most famous stories is "The Tell-Tale Heart." In this story, the narrator is drawn to kill and later to confess his crime. Poe also published a collection of stories called *Tales of the Grotesque and Arabesque.* Many of his stories involve plots of revenge and murder. The fear of death, especially of being buried alive, is a common theme. His most famous poem was "The Raven." Many people have enjoyed reading Poe's horrifying tales.

2)
> Regular exercise keeps a person fit. People who exercise feel better and probably live longer. Exercise also helps people to maintain a healthy weight. It stimulates the heart and lungs. After a person exercises, he or she will probably be sore and tired. Everyone should try to exercise every day.

3)
> Our camping trip was simply awful! We froze at night and chased bugs away all day. No one caught a single fish! We enjoyed hiking through the woods. It took us an hour to start a fire, and the dinner burned. The strong winds overturned one canoe and blew down two tents. On top of it all, it rained. I am sure that we will never plan another camping trip.

Combining Paragraphs

The number of sentences in the body of a paragraph will vary. Sometimes you may find that you have written two or three short paragraphs about the same main idea. Combine those paragraphs into one longer one.

Activity D   Read the two short paragraphs below. Both are about the same topic. Combine the two paragraphs into one longer paragraph. Follow these steps:

1) Write a new topic sentence.
2) Use details and facts from both paragraphs to write new sentences.
3) Write the new paragraph on your paper. Remember to indent the first word of the topic sentence.

> Springfield used to be a small town. The population is growing. Springfield is now larger than some cities.
> Many people are moving to Springfield. Older people find that it is a quiet and pleasant place to live. Many recreational activities attract young, active families. Jobs are plentiful. Large, older homes are affordable. Someday, Springfield may become a city.

Use the body of a paragraph to develop your main idea.

- The body is the middle part of a paragraph.
- The body is made of one or more sentences.
- The sentences of the body support the main idea of the paragraph.
- The body of a paragraph can include facts, details, explanations, reasons, examples, and illustrations.

Part A   Read the three paragraphs below. Copy the one sentence that does not support each paragraph. Explain why this sentence does not belong with the rest of its paragraph.

1) You would like my friend, Ms. Lentz. She is almost always cheerful and friendly. Ms. Lentz owns a gas station. I like to stop by her home to visit. She invites me in for a snack. We always have fascinating conversations. A visit to Ms. Lentz brightens my day.

2) Amanda's mother likes to read. She also goes to dancing class with Amanda. Her favorite books are mysteries. She enjoys hunting for clues. Sometimes she likes to read short stories. They allow her to visit other times and places without leaving her house. She says that reading is relaxing, informative, and fun.

3) Lemonade is a refreshing drink. If freshly squeezed lemons are used, lemonade has vitamin C. We add sugar to our lemonade. Too much sugar is not good for you. Lemonade tastes best on a hot summer day.

Part B   Choose one of the sample topic sentences below, or write a topic sentence of your own. Then write three sentences that support the topic. Be sure to indent the first line.

- A funny thing happened today before school.
- Before buying a computer, think about these three points.
- Daily exercise is important for good health.

Summary

A statement that briefly repeats main points, often as the last sentence of a paragraph or the last sentences of an essay.

How will you bring your paragraph to a close? You might write a sentence that gives a **summary**. A summary is a statement that briefly repeats the main idea of the paragraph. A summary sentence does not add information to the paragraph. It repeats the main idea using slightly different words. A summary is to a paragraph what a period is to a sentence. They both announce, "The end."

Read this paragraph. Notice how the last sentence repeats the main idea in slightly different words. The last sentence is a summary.

> Track has become Derek's favorite activity. He runs five miles every day and goes to practice regularly. He has won three races already. Derek will continue to improve his time, according to his coach. Derek is working hard at track and enjoying it, too.

Conclusion

A logical judgment based on evidence; often presented at the end of a paragraph or an essay.

Another way to end a paragraph is with a **conclusion**. A conclusion is a judgment based on the facts or evidence that you presented in the paragraph. A conclusion must be logical. It must make sense.

The paragraph above could end with a conclusion instead of a summary sentence. This conclusion could replace the last sentence: *Derek has a good chance to win a college scholarship in track.*

Activity A   Read each paragraph. Write a summary sentence for each one.

1) In today's world, education must never stop. New scientific discoveries appear almost daily. The jobs that must be done keep changing. The amount of new information that people need to know is increasing rapidly!

2) Springtime is my favorite season of the year. The air has a pleasant scent. Flowers and trees are budding. Birds are nesting. The world seems suddenly colorful. I feel like spending more time outdoors.

Activity B Read the two paragraphs below. Study the last sentence of each. Does paragraph 1 or paragraph 2 have a logical conclusion? Write a sentence on your paper to give a reason for your choice.

1) Amanda and Laura wondered whether Saturday would be a good day for a picnic. Most of their friends were going away. The weather forecast called for rain. All week the weather had been cold. They decided to postpone the picnic until some other time.

2) Last year Amanda's mother bought a computer for Amanda. Amanda and her mother enjoyed playing computer games. Ms. O'Hara used the computer to keep track of spending. Amanda used the computer to learn Spanish. The computer had been a waste of money.

Activity C Read both of the paragraphs below. Read the last sentence of each paragraph carefully. Decide whether that ending sentence is a summary or a conclusion. On your paper, write *Summary* or *Conclusion*.

1) Every day, Ms. Lentz listens to the weather report. Then she looks outside. One day the report called for sunny skies. The chance of rain was only ten percent. When Ms. Lentz looked outside, she saw that it was raining. She decided that the weather report was wrong.

2) Ms. Lentz does the same thing every morning. She gets up, takes a shower, gets dressed, and then reads her newspaper. While she eats her breakfast, she reads. When she has finished the paper, she leaves for work. Ms. Lentz follows this routine every day.

You can bring a paragraph to a close by writing a final sentence. The sentence can be a summary or a conclusion.

- A summary states the main idea again but with different words.
- A conclusion is a logical judgment based on the details in the paragraph.

Part A Read each paragraph below. End the first paragraph with a summary statement. End the second with a conclusion.

1) Have you ever found a writer who makes you laugh out loud? I read everything I can find by Dave Barry. Every week, I read his column in the newspaper. If it is especially funny, I cut it out and save it. I have also bought two of Dave Barry's books.

2) The Summer Olympics includes a contest called the decathlon. The decathlon is actually ten events. Athletes from all over the world try to run fastest in the 100-meter, the 400-meter, and the 1,500-meter races. They run a high hurdle race. They throw the discus, the javelin, and the shot put. They leap in the high jump and the long jump. They also aim high in the pole vault.

Part B Read the paragraphs below. Write either a summary or a conclusion for each paragraph.

1) Last month, Derek met a girl on the track team. She runs the mile. She told him that she has played sports all her life. She also teaches an exercise class. She and Derek share many interests. Her name is Shirley.

2) Amanda and Laura are worried about their friend Derek. Now that he has met Shirley, he looks dreamy all the time. He has stopped doing his homework. His old friends hardly ever see him.

Part A Write a topic sentence that could introduce a paragraph on each topic below.

1) A dangerous job

2) Something of value

3) The perfect car

4) Schools of the future

5) Fame

Part B Read each set of four facts below and on the next page. Use each set of facts to write a paragraph. Add more information if you wish. Start your paragraph with a topic sentence. End your paragraph with a summary or a conclusion.

1) People use personal computers for word processing.

   Personal computers connect users to other computers.

   Students do research using personal computers.

   People do their taxes on personal computers.

2) Visitors want to see the steep canyon walls.

   Rafting trips down the river are popular.

   Mules take riders to the bottom of the canyon.

   There are many hiking trails.

3) An encyclopedia gives general information.

   A dictionary gives word meanings.

   A dictionary also gives word histories.

   An atlas contains maps.

4) First roll out the dough for the crust.

Place the dough in a pie plate.

Next prepare the filling.

Pour the filling into the crust.

5) Snow began falling at midnight.

It continued to fall for 36 hours.

Snow piled high in the streets.

No cars were allowed downtown.

Part C   Read the paragraphs below. Write a summary or a conclusion for each paragraph.

1) Mike's little brother, Tim, loves tennis. Although he is very young, Tim is strong. He moves quickly around the court. He has developed a spin serve. His two-handed backhand is steady.

2) There are six children in Mike's family. Mike is the oldest. Next in line is his sister, Karen. The middle kids are twins. Their names are Jack and Joe. Number five is Kathy. The youngest child is Tim.

Part D   Write a five-sentence paragraph on this topic:
The three parts of a paragraph.

Test Taking Tip   Look over a test before you begin answering questions. See how many parts there are. See what you are being asked to do on each part.

Chapter 8

The Purpose of a Paragraph

Think about the purpose of your last piece of writing. Were you writing to explain an idea? Maybe you were asking for information. Maybe you were giving directions. You might have been writing to express your opinion.

You write for all sorts of purposes. No matter what your purpose is, you use paragraphs to organize your ideas. Paragraphs make your ideas clear to your readers.

In Chapter 8, you will learn about common purposes of paragraphs. You will practice writing paragraphs for different purposes.

Goals for Learning

▶ To write a paragraph that informs and explains

▶ To write a paragraph that explains how to do something

▶ To write a paragraph that makes a request

▶ To write a paragraph that persuades

▶ To write a paragraph that tells a story

When you write to inform and explain, you give your readers facts about a topic. In your paragraph, you aim for one or more of these goals:

- To make something clear

- To help someone understand an idea

- To give the meaning of something

- To give reasons for something

Your topic sentence prepares your readers for your main idea. The body of your paragraph is made of sentences that give facts and other supporting details. Your final sentence may be a summary or a conclusion.

Activity A   This paragraph gives information. Read it. Then write answers to the questions on your paper.

The Personal Computer

Personal computers are appearing in more and more homes. Even the smallest personal computers are more powerful than the room-sized computers of the 1960s. Computers have become easy and fun to use. Families use computers to find information, write letters, play games, draw pictures, save a mailing list, and keep track of checkbook balances. Someday soon, people will not remember a time when they did not have computers in their homes.

---

1) What is the main idea of this paragraph? Use your own words to state the main idea.

2) What facts and reasons does the writer give to support the main idea?

3) What conclusion does the writer give? Use your own words to state the conclusion.

Paragraphs Based on Definitions

You may write a paragraph that develops a definition. Use details from dictionaries and encyclopedias to write a paragraph that informs and explains.

Compare the definition below with the paragraph that is based on it.

> **EXAMPLES**   Definition:
>
> **Killiecrankie** *(n.)* a mountain pass in Scotland; the place where a battle was fought in 1689.
>
> Paragraph:
>
>   Have you ever heard of Killiecrankie? Killiecrankie is the name of a place in Scotland. It is a mountain pass. In 1689, a famous battle was fought there. Killiecrankie would be an interesting place to visit.

Activity B   Read the following words and meanings. Use each definition to write a short paragraph about the word. Start with a topic sentence. End your paragraph with a summary or a conclusion.

1) **glockenspiel** *(n.)* an instrument with flat level bars, formerly bells or tubes, set in a frame; the metal bars are tuned to produce bell-like tones when struck with two small hammers. It is a percussion instrument.

2) **paisley** *(adj.)* a type of cloth with a colorful pattern of flowers or designs; originally used to make soft wool shawls. This pattern is named after Paisley, Scotland, where it was first made.

3) **leotard** *(n.)* a tight-fitting garment made of a stretchy fabric. It is worn by dancers, gymnasts, and people who are exercising. It is named for a nineteenth-century French acrobat, Jules Léotard, who wore the garment and made it famous.

4) **doodle** *(v.)* to wander aimlessly or without purpose; also, to scribble designs on a piece of paper. To doodle originally meant to play a bagpipe.

Answering Questions

Informative paragraphs can answer questions. If a question asks *why*, you can answer it with an explanation. Your paragraph tells about causes. You give statements to prove the idea is right.

Read the question below. Notice how the paragraph gives an explanation to answer the question.

EXAMPLE

Question:

Why did Othello kill Desdemona?

Paragraph answer:

In Shakespeare's play, Othello killed his wife, Desdemona, because of a mistake. Othello's false friend, Iago, lied to him. Iago told Othello that Desdemona was in love with another man. Othello was in a rage. To get revenge, he smothered his innocent wife. Othello found out that he was wrong. But it was too late to undo the terrible mistake.

Activity C   Choose one of the questions below. Write a paragraph to answer it.

- What is your favorite sport, and why do you prefer it?

- Why is a good education important for everyone?

- What is your favorite television show, and why do you like it?

- Why do people do things that they later regret?

- Why is it important to be on time?

You may write a paragraph to give information or explain an idea.

- Make your main idea clear in a topic sentence.
- Use the body of the paragraph to give facts and reasons.
- End with a conclusion or a summary.

Part A   Read the paragraph below. Then answer the questions that follow it on your paper.

Who's Who

When you write a report, you may want to get information from *Who's Who*. This commonly used reference book lists the names of famous living people. The names are listed in alphabetic order. A short paragraph is included about each person. This paragraph is a brief biography and gives a few facts about the person's life. A little information about many people can be found in *Who's Who*.

---

1) What is the main idea of this paragraph?

2) What information would you find in *Who's Who?*

3) What are three facts about *Who's Who?*

4) What is the purpose of the last sentence?

Part B   Write a paragraph on one of the topics listed below. State the main idea in the first sentence. Write three sentences that give facts and reasons to support the main idea. End with a summary or conclusion. Your completed paragraph should have five sentences.

- Uses for a dictionary
- What is a friend?
- What makes a good movie?
- The meaning of *silhouette*

The shelves of libraries are filled with how-to books. They tell readers how to do something or how to make something. You can tell your readers how to do or make something, too. Write a paragraph that clearly explains the steps to follow.

In a how-to paragraph, your topic sentence should tell readers what they will be doing or making. The body of the paragraph takes them through the steps with words such as *first, next, when*, and *finally*. Your final sentence can be a conclusion or a summary.

Activity A   Read the how-to paragraph below. Then answer the questions that follow on your paper.

Blowout!

If your car tire suddenly loses air while you are driving, what should you do? The first thing to do is stay calm. The car may be swerving, but do not step on the brake. Instead, keep your foot steady on the gas pedal. At the same time, hold the steering wheel firmly. Next, turn on your hazard lights. When the swerving lessens, slowly take your foot off the gas pedal. Finally, steer gently to the shoulder of the road. Your goal is to get the car off the road safely.

---

1) What is the main idea of this paragraph?

2) What words help the reader know when to take certain steps?

3) What is another way of stating the final sentence?

Activity B   You have invited a friend home for dinner. Write a paragraph that gives him or her directions from school to your home.

Proofread

To look for mistakes in spelling, grammar, punctuation, and other things.

Revise

To correct errors or to make changes.

Rewrite

To write again.

Proofreading and Revising Paragraphs

After you have written a paragraph, look for ways to improve it. To **proofread** your paragraph, look for mistakes in spelling, grammar, and punctuation. To **revise** your paragraph, correct any errors. Make other improvements. You may need to **rewrite** your paragraph.

Use this checklist when you look over your paragraphs.

Checklist for Proofreading and Revising a Paragraph

1. Do you have a meaningful title?
2. Is the first line of your paragraph indented? Does it start on a new line?
3. Does your topic sentence prepare the reader for the main idea of your paragraph?
4. Do the sentences in the body of the paragraph support the main idea? Have you included facts, details, explanations, reasons, examples, or illustrations? Have you taken out any sentences that do not relate to your main idea?
5. Do you have a conclusion or a summary at the end?
6. Read each sentence carefully. Does each sentence have a capital letter and a correct end punctuation mark? Does each sentence have a subject and a verb? Does each sentence express a complete thought? Correct any run-on sentences.
7. Can you improve your sentences? Can you add specific and vivid adjectives, adverbs, or prepositional phrases? Can you combine short, related ideas into longer, more varied sentences?
8. Check the following items in your paragraph. Correct any errors that you find. (You can look up these topics in the index of this book.)

   - Spelling
   - Punctuation
   - Capitalization of proper nouns
   - Subject-verb agreement
   - Agreement of pronouns and antecedents
   - Tenses and spellings of irregular verbs
   - Spellings of plurals and possessives

Activity C Practice using the checklist in this lesson. Read the how-to paragraph below. Proofread for mistakes. Revise by changing the order of some sentences. You may want to combine short sentences into longer ones. Rewrite the improved paragraph on your paper.

How to Have a Successful Garden

To have a succesful garden you must do several things. Following all of these steps will guarantee you a rich harvest First, you must chose the right spot, the garden will need plenty of sunshine. It helps to have a slight slope for good drainage. Its also a good idea to fertilize. Be sure to buy good seeds. Water and weed your garden. Plant your seeds. Later, you will be able to enjoy the fruits of your labor.

Activity D Sometimes a friend can be a helpful proofreader and adviser. Choose one of the paragraphs you have written so far in this chapter. Then take these steps:

1) Exchange paragraphs with a partner.

2) Proofread each other's paragraphs.

3) Offer suggestions for revising.

4) Rewrite your own paragraph.

A how-to paragraph explains to readers how to do or make something. Your paragraph should include these three main parts:

- topic sentence

- body

- conclusion or summary

Part A   The following facts tell how to become more physically fit. Use the facts to write a how-to paragraph. Start with your own topic sentence. Rewrite the sentences below. Use words such as *first* and *finally* to make the steps clear. Add a conclusion or a summary at the end of your paragraph. Use the checklist on page 185 to proofread and revise your paragraph.

1) Build the activity into your schedule.

2) Start with a short walk around the block.

3) Take the walk several times a week.

4) Gradually increase your walking speed.

5) Work up to a fast mile-and-a-half walk three times a week.

Part B   Think of something that you know how to do. Write a paragraph about that topic. Follow these directions:

1) Write no more than seven sentences.

2) Make the first sentence a topic sentence.

3) Make the last sentence a summary.

Use the checklist on page 185 to proofread and revise your paragraph.

You may write a paragraph to ask for information. Use the body of the paragraph to explain the main idea of your request. Read this sample letter.

Dear Sir or Madam:

Please send me information about *Video View*. How often is this magazine published? What is the price of a subscription? I would like to look at a copy of the magazine. Where can I find one? Thank you for your help.

Sincerely,

Amanda O'Hara

Amanda O'Hara

Activity A Answer the following questions about this letter.

1) What is the main idea of this paragraph?

2) What exactly does Amanda want to know about the magazine?

3) How does Amanda end the paragraph?

Activity B Write a paragraph asking for specific information. Choose one of the topic sentences below. Add three sentences that explain the request in more detail. Think carefully about the specific information that you would need to know. Add a conclusion.

- I am seeking information about vacations on a cruise ship.
- Please tell me more about your party.
- Please send me information about your stereo equipment.
- I need some information about growing vegetables.

Clear, Specific Requests

When you are writing to request information, be specific. If your question is vague, the response may be incomplete.

Suppose that someone is asking Derek about his new friend, Shirley. A vague question may produce a vague answer.

EXAMPLE

Vague question: Who is Shirley?

Vague answer: She's a girl I know.

Compare the more specific request with the more complete response.

EXAMPLE

Specific request:

I would like to know about your new friend, Shirley. Where did you meet her? What does she like to do? Tell me about her family. I would like to hear all about Shirley.

Specific answer:

Shirley is the most wonderful girl I have ever met. We are both on the track team. She runs the mile. Shirley has one older brother. Her mother works at the supermarket. Her dad is a carpenter. You will like Shirley when you meet her.

Activity C   Choose a partner in your class. Then follow these directions.

1) Write a paragraph requesting information about your partner. Be specific in your request.

2) Exchange paragraphs with your partner.

3) Write a second paragraph that answers the questions your partner asked. Be specific in your answers.

When you ask for information, be specific. Ask a clear question, and you will get a clear answer.

Part A   Each of these questions is vague. Rewrite each one to ask a more specific question.

Example   Vague question: What is the price of your vacuum cleaner?

Specific question: What is the price of the Model 4150 Deluxe Canister vacuum cleaner?

1) What is Mexico like?

2) Do you have any information about computers?

3) Is Springfield a good place to live?

4) How do I get to Centerville?

5) What is the job?

Part B   Rewrite this paragraph so that the request is clear and specific.

> I saw your ad for an apartment. I am interested in renting it. Please tell me more about it.

Persuade

To write or talk in a convincing way; to give reasons and facts that convince others to act or believe in a certain way; to appeal to feelings in order to convince.

Do you have a good idea? Would you like to convince someone else that your idea will work? Then write to **persuade**. When you persuade readers, they will believe what you tell them. They will act in the way you suggest.

To write a persuasive paragraph, keep these points in mind:

- State your position or your request clearly.
- Use logical reasons to support your position.
- Use facts to support your position.
- Think about your reader's doubts. Try to overcome those doubts.

Suppose that Derek is applying for a scholarship to Western College. The application form includes a question asking why he thinks he deserves a scholarship. Read the paragraph that Derek writes in response to that question.

I believe that I deserve a scholarship to Western College. I participate fully in school events. My major activity at Springfield High School is the track team. I intend to continue running track in college. I know that Western College has high academic standards, and I look forward to the opportunity to learn. Although I was only a fair student when I began high school, I began to challenge myself at the end of my sophomore year. My grades have improved steadily. I work hard and take my studies seriously. I need this scholarship to continue my education. I hope you agree that I would be a successful and involved student at Western College.

Activity A   Answer these questions about Derek's paragraph.

1) Whom is Derek trying to persuade in this paragraph?

2) What is he trying to persuade his readers to do?

3) What objection has he noted and overcome in his paragraph?

Suppose that Mike believes that he and his friend Derek can win the next tennis tournament. Listed below are the reasons that Mike will give to persuade Derek to play in the tournament.

Mike's Reasons

1. I have been practicing.
2. I have developed a better serve.
3. I will practice with Derek every day.
4. We both have had experience; we will not be as nervous as we were last time.
5. The other players are not very good.
6. I have a strong wish to enter the tournament.

Activity B   Pretend that you are Mike. Use the reasons above to write a persuasive paragraph. Try to persuade Derek to join you as a partner in the next tennis tournament.

1) Start with a topic sentence. State your request or position.

2) Include the reasons in the body of your paragraph.

3) End the paragraph with a summary or conclusion.

4) Proofread, revise, and rewrite your paragraph. Use the checklist on page 185.

Activity C Derek wants to persuade Mike to find another partner. Write a paragraph for Derek. Follow the directions below.

1) Be sure that your paragraph begins with a topic sentence.

2) Think of logical reasons why Mike should find another partner. Be convincing. Give facts. Be creative.

3) End your paragraph with a summary or a conclusion.

4) Add a title to your paragraph.

5) Proofread, revise, and rewrite your paragraph. Use the checklist on page 185.

Sometimes you want your readers to act or to believe in a certain way. Write a paragraph of persuasion.

- State your main idea in a topic sentence.

- Use facts and reasons to support your main idea.

- Use your last sentence to sum up your case.

Lesson Review   Write a paragraph of persuasion. Follow the directions.

1) Choose one of these topics. Use it as the title of your paragraph. You may make up your own topic instead.

- Why Every School Should Have a Technology Center

- Why Everyone Should Exercise

- Summer: The Best Season of the Year

- Why I Should Be Hired for the Job of (Name of Job)

2) Write your paragraph. State your main idea in a topic sentence. Persuade by giving reasons and facts in the body of your paragraph. End your paragraph with a summary or a conclusion.

3) Finally, proofread, revise, and rewrite your paragraph. Refer to the checklist on page 185.

Anecdote

A very short story about an interesting or amusing happening.

Fiction

An imaginary story; writing based largely on the writer's imagination.

Nonfiction

Writing that expresses facts and ideas; a true story, rather than an imaginary one.

Personal Narrative

A true story told from the viewpoint of the narrator.

When you write a story, you are answering a basic question: "What happened?" Stories come in different sizes. A story may be one thousand pages long. A story may be only one paragraph long. A story that short is sometimes called an **anecdote**.

Stories can be **fiction**, or based on an author's imagination. Stories can be **nonfiction**, or based on actual events and real people. A true story that uses the pronouns *I* and *me* is called a **personal narrative**.

Activity A   Read the following paragraph. Write your answers to the questions that follow it on your paper.

The Day I Almost Drowned
by Laura Gonzales

When I was eight years old, I almost drowned in the Gulf of Mexico. My cousin Julio and I were playing with a raft. Suddenly, he let go. The raft started to drift out to sea. It was a windy day, but I did not want to lose the raft. As I swam toward the raft, the wind took it out farther and farther. Soon I was out too far. I could not get back to shore. People were yelling, but I could not hear them. A man on shore saw me and swam out to rescue me. When I got back to the beach, my mom and Julio were crying. We all thanked the man who had saved me from drowning. Almost drowning was an unforgettable experience!

---

1) Who is the "I" of this story?

2) Who are the other characters or people in this story?

3) What event does this paragraph tell about?

4) Assume that Laura is a real person. Is her story fiction or nonfiction?

Activity B   Write a paragraph that tells a story about something that happened to you.

1) Begin with a topic sentence.

2) Use the body to tell the beginning, middle, and end of your story.

3) End the paragraph with a comment on your feelings about your experience.

Dialogue

Stories often include dialogue, the exact words spoken by people or characters. If you include dialogue in your story, then you will set up the paragraphs differently. Remember that each time the speaker changes, you must begin a new paragraph. Remember to enclose the speaker's exact words in quotation marks.

Activity C   Read the story below. Then write your answers to the questions that follow it on your paper.

My Luckiest Day

By Marta Gonzales

"Laura! Laura! Let the raft go! You are out too far!" I screamed to my daughter.

"I'm sorry, Aunt Marta," Julio cried.

"Do you want me to go out and get her?" asked a stranger.

"Oh, yes," I said. The man jumped into the water at once. In a few minutes, Laura and the man were back on the shore.

"Thank you!" I cried. Then I ran to hug Laura.

When I looked around a moment later, the man was gone. I wish that I could have thanked him more.

---

1) Who is telling this story?

2) How many paragraphs are there?

3) How many times does Marta Gonzales speak?

4) How many times does Julio speak?

5) What are the exact words spoken by the stranger?

6) How is this second story different from the one titled "The Day I Almost Drowned" on page 194?

Chronological Order

When you write paragraphs to tell a story, you must think about the order of events. Often, you will tell about events in **chronological order**, the order in which they happened. You may start with the oldest event and end with the most recent.

Notice the chronological order in this paragraph about an event.

How I Met Shirley
by Derek Corelli

One day last month, I was running laps at the track. I wasn't watching where I was going. I bumped into another runner. We really bumped! We both fell. Each of us saw the other's surprised face at the same moment and started laughing. I noticed immediately that the other runner had a beautiful smile. She told me her name was Shirley. After practice, we started talking. Soon we decided to meet for practice after school three days a week.

Activity D   Write the answers to these questions about Derek's paragraph.

1) When did the event take place?

2) What happened right after Derek and Shirley bumped into each other?

3) Why did they both start laughing?

4) What was the last thing that happened?

Activity E   Write a paragraph about historical events. Read the list of events below. Use them to tell the story of St. Paul, Minnesota. Start with the oldest event and end with the most recent.

- St. Paul became a city in 1854.
- The name of the settlement was changed to St. Paul in 1841, when Father Lucien Galtier built St. Paul's Chapel.
- It became a town in 1849.
- The settlement was first named "Pig's Eye" after its first European settler, Pierre "Pig's Eye" Parrant.

Paragraphs that tell a story answer the question, "What happened?"

- A story may be fiction or nonfiction.
- A story has a beginning, a middle, and an end.
- Think about chronological order. Report events in the order in which they happened.

Part A   Read the paragraph below. Then write your answers to the questions that follow on your paper.

> My life began in Springfield about seven years ago. I had three sisters, but they were all sold. Amanda and her mother wanted to keep me, so I wasn't sold. Now I spend my days eating, sleeping, and barking. Whenever I get a chance, I jump the fence and run away. Everyone chases me and yells, "Benjy!" It is a lot of fun. All in all, I'm a happy guy.

1) What words point out chronological order in this paragraph?

2) What is the purpose of the final sentence?

3) What would be a good title for this paragraph?

Part B   Read each of the sentences below. Think about stories that each one suggests. Then choose one idea for a story. Develop and write a story of one paragraph or more. Use dialogue if you wish. Remember to proofread, revise, and rewrite your story. Refer to the checklist on page 185.

- I had a weird experience.
- Did I do the right thing?
- Some moments are unforgettable.
- The incident made everyone laugh.

Part A   Each topic sentence below could lead into a paragraph. Write what main purpose each paragraph would serve. Choose from these purposes:

- to inform or explain
- to persuade
- to make a request
- to tell a story

1) Last Friday evening began like any other Friday evening.

2) I would like information about the drummers' workshop being offered by Driscoll College.

3) Karli Lane deserves your vote for council president.

4) You can learn the right way to wash a car.

5) Basketball players need special abilities.

Now choose one of the five topic sentences. Write a paragraph that begins with that topic sentence. Add at least three sentences to the body of the paragraph. End the paragraph with a conclusion or a summary. Then proofread and revise your paragraph.

Part B   Proofread the paragraph below to find errors. Rewrite the paragraph correctly on your paper.

My Busy Life
by Derek Corelli

Lately, it is hard to fit in all of my activites. Three days each week, I work for a few hours in the evening at Ms. Lentz' gas station. Every day from Monday to friday, I go to school. After school I have track practice. My girlfriend Shirley and I run some evenings as well on the weekends. Often I get up early to do homework before i leave for school. My mother keeps saying aren't you overdoing things, Derek?

Part C   Read the five sets of directions below. Choose **three** of them to follow. Write three paragraphs. Remember to proofread and revise.

1) Write a paragraph that gives information about a person, animal, place, or thing. You may use one of these topics if you wish.

- A sports hero
- A popular place
- An unusual bird
- The ideal room
- The climate in your region

2) Write a paragraph that tells a reader how to make or do something. You may use one of these topics if you wish.

- How to change the oil in a car
- How to write a paragraph
- How to celebrate a birthday
- How to solve a problem
- How to cook a certain food

3) Write a paragraph in which you ask for information. You may be asking about a product, a service, a place, or anything you wish. Be specific in your request.

4) Write a paragraph in which you persuade your reader to give you something that you want. Start by thinking about what you want. For example, you might want an *A* in English, a car, a new coat, or a scholarship. Then think about the person you wish to convince. Persuade this person that you deserve the item you have selected.

5) Write a paragraph that tells a story. The story may be fiction or nonfiction. Tell what happened by putting the events in chronological order.

Test Taking Tip | When a test item asks you to write a paragraph, make a plan first. Jot down the main idea of your paragraph. List the supporting details you can include. Then write the paragraph.

Chapter 9

Improving Your Paragraphs

Suppose that you hear about a person who always "does things with style." That person probably uses imagination. That person probably tries to do things in lively, uncommon ways. A person with style is interesting to meet.

Be a writer who "does things with style." Your writing will be interesting to read. Give your paragraphs style by making them lively. Use words and sentences in varied, appealing ways.

You have learned about writing clear, correct paragraphs. Now you can try making those paragraphs even better. In this chapter, you will learn how to improve your paragraphs.

Goals for Learning

▶ To improve topic sentences

▶ To use sentence variety

▶ To make smooth transitions between sentences

▶ To make comparisons

You have learned that a topic sentence prepares your reader for the main idea of your paragraph. A topic sentence can also get a reader's attention. A lively topic sentence makes the reader want to find out more.

To improve a topic sentence, get to the point. Take out unnecessary words. Add information that will grab the reader's attention. Compare the topic sentences below.

EXAMPLE   Poor: Let me begin by telling about New Orleans, which is an interesting place to visit.

Better: New Orleans is a one-of-a-kind city that offers visitors experiences they will never forget.

Activity A   These topic sentences need improvement. Rewrite them by taking out unnecessary words. Add words that will grab a reader's attention.

1) This paragraph is about our family vacation in Arizona.

2) I think I will begin this paragraph by telling you that I just got a new CD player.

3) Let me tell you about what I want to be someday, which is a musician.

4) I am going to write about the trip my friends and I took to a museum last Saturday.

One way to get your reader's attention is by asking a question. Notice the topic sentence in the paragraph below. It asks a question.

Cologne

Have you ever wondered how cologne got its name? Cologne is a fragrant liquid that is used like perfume. It was first made in a city in Germany over 200 years ago. The name of the city is Cologne! Its famous product became known by the French name *Eau de Cologne*, which translates as "water of cologne." The name has been shortened to *cologne*.

Activity B Read each pair of questions below. Decide which one is better as a topic sentence. Write *a* or *b* as your answer. Be ready to give reasons for your choice.

1) a) Would you like me to tell you something about my cat?
   b) Have you met Harold, our family cat?

2) a) Aren't some plants interesting?
   b) Have you ever heard of a meat-eating plant?

3) a) Would you like to live next door to a volcano?
   b) What is a volcano?

Activity C Write a short paragraph. Choose your own topic. Begin your paragraph with a question. The topic sentence should get to the point. It should get a reader's attention.

Point of View

Point of view *An opinion; the way in which something is looked at.*	You may use your topic sentence to express your opinion. Give your readers your **point of view**. Help them to see your way of looking at the topic.

Include enough information in your topic sentence. Your topic sentence should lead your reader into the body of your paragraph. The body gives supporting details about your point of view.

EXAMPLE Poor: Some television shows are boring.

Better: Television shows about roommates are all alike.

Activity D Write a topic sentence for each topic below. Express a point of view. Include enough information to lead the reader into your paragraph.

1) Going to the doctor
2) Eating pickles
3) Thanksgiving dinner
4) Poison ivy
5) Oatmeal
6) Personal computers

A topic sentence prepares a reader for the main idea of a paragraph. A lively topic sentence grabs the reader's attention. He or she wants to read on to find out more.

- A topic sentence should get to the point.
- A topic sentence may ask a question.
- A topic sentence may express a point of view.

Part A   Read each pair of topic sentences below. Which one is better? Write *a* or *b* as your answer. Write a short explanation for your choice.

1) **a)** This paragraph is going to be about my cat.
   b) Our cat, Harold, rules our home with an iron paw.

2) **a)** Derek Corelli is a student who runs track at Springfield High School.
   b) Meet Derek Corelli, a shining star of Springfield High's track team.

3) **a)** Have you ever read a book with 1,037 pages?
   b) *Gone With the Wind* is about the Civil War.

4) **a)** Cigarettes are weapons of death.
   b) Cigarette smoking is bad for your health.

5) **a)** One day at the beach, a terrible tragedy almost took place.
   b) I'm going to tell you about a dangerous experience I had at the beach.

Part B   Each topic sentence below needs improvement. Rewrite each one to make it better.

1) We saw a movie not long ago.

2) Let me tell you about a funny dream I had once.

3) Do you know what is really boring?

4) Science can be an interesting subject.

5) The book I read was about motorcycles.

> Variety's the very spice of life,
> That gives it all its flavor.
>
> —William Cowper

Variety

A number or collection of many different things.

Spice up your paragraphs by giving your sentences **variety**. Sentences with variety are more interesting to read. Here are some ways to add variety to sentences:

- Start sentences with adverbs.
- Start sentences with prepositional phrases.
- Make your sentences different lengths. Some can be short. Others can be long.

Activity A   Rewrite the sentences below. Combine each pair of sentences into one longer sentence. Use a conjunction. Add necessary punctuation. If you wish, review the lesson on combining sentences, on pages 151–159.

Example   Two sentences: Mike was excited about the tennis match. Derek was worried.

Combined: Mike was excited about the tennis match, but Derek was worried.

1) After the tennis match, Mike was happy. Derek was tired.

2) Derek wanted to go home. Mike wanted to celebrate.

3) Mike wants to play in another tournament. Derek does not.

4) Derek and Mike are good friends. Derek just does not like tennis.

Activity B   Rewrite these sentences. Begin each sentence with an adverb or a prepositional phrase. If you wish, review the lessons on pages 132–150.

Examples   Sentence: Derek has the better forehand.

Improved: Surprisingly, Derek has the better forehand. (adverb added)

Improved: Of the two friends, Derek has the better forehand. (prepositional phrase added)

1) Mike's tennis serve is better.

2) Their friends cheered when Mike and Derek won.

3) The tournament director gave them a trophy.

4) Mike has been showing everyone the trophy.

5) Derek hopes that this tournament is his last.

Activity C   Read Mike's paragraph below. Then improve it by taking the steps that follow. Rewrite the paragraph with your changes.

The Tennis Match

The story that I am about to tell is about an important tennis match. The match began at noon. The sun was very hot that day. The hopes were high that Derek and I would win. The opponents were weak and out of shape. The match ended differently from the others. The victory this time was ours!

---

1) All the sentences start with the same word, *The*. Vary the sentence beginnings.

2) Add or change words to make the sentences livelier.

3) Combine two short sentences into a longer sentence. Use a conjunction. Punctuate the new sentence correctly.

When you read over your paragraphs, look for ways to add variety. Make your sentences more interesting for your readers.

- Begin your sentences with different words, including adverbs and prepositional phrases.

- Combine some short sentences to make longer ones.

Part A   Read the news item below. Then rewrite it on your own paper. Add variety to the sentences.

KAPLAN AND CORELLI WIN TENNIS TOURNAMENT

The Annual Springfield Tennis Tournament had a surprise ending. The Harris twins were the defending champions. The guys looked tired and out of shape. The challengers were a new pair named Mike Kaplan and Derek Corelli They took command immediately. The final scores were 6–0 and 6–2.

Part B   Choose one of the suggested topics below, or use one of your own topics. Write a paragraph about your chosen topic. Aim for sentence variety!

- Describe a recent sporting event.

- Tell about your favorite sport or hobby.

- Explain why you prefer a particular kind of music.

- Write a review of a movie that you have seen recently.

Transition

An expression that connects ideas, sentences, or paragraphs (however, therefore, on the other hand, in the meantime).

You can improve your paragraphs by making smooth, clear connections among the ideas in your sentences. Try using words such as *as a result, finally, on the other hand,* and *meanwhile.* Such words and expressions are called **transitions**. They help your reader see how your ideas are related.

Use these transitions to show connections in time.

While	Later
Meanwhile	Soon
Then	At last
Finally	Next
In the meantime	Before
At the end	First

EXAMPLE

Connection not clear:
No rain fell for three months. Thunderclouds appeared.

Connection clear with transition:
No rain fell for three months. At last, thunderclouds appeared.

Study the list of transitions below. Transitions such as *also* and *in addition* point out how things are alike. Transitions such as *however* and *on the other hand* point out differences. Transitions such as *in conclusion* and *therefore* point out causes and results. All transitions show connections among ideas.

However	In conclusion
For example	As a result
Also	Consequently
Furthermore	Therefore
In addition	

Connection not clear:
A personal computer has many uses. Children use software to learn math and reading.

Connection clear with transition:
A personal computer has many uses. For example, children use software to learn math and reading.

Activity A Read the paragraph below. Notice how transitions make connections smooth and clear. List the transitions that you find. (Not every sentence will have one.)

Cable TV Comes Home!
by Amanda O'Hara

For a long time, I have wanted cable television. After much discussion, my mother agreed to sign up. At last it is here! We used to get seven television channels. Now we get 70! Our family, however, has only one television set. Therefore, every evening we have long talks about what to watch. Sometimes it is hard for us to agree on one channel. Cable television has both advantages and disadvantages for my family.

Activity B Practice using transitions. Rewrite the paragraph below. Improve it by adding some of the transitions listed on page 208.

A Good Night's Sleep

Would you like to improve the quality of your sleep? Give yourself a bedtime routine. Do something relaxing. Read a book. Listen to soothing music. Take a bath. Go to bed at the same time. Wake up at the same time. You will feel more rested.

Transitions are words that connect ideas in sentences. Use transitions to take your reader smoothly from one idea to another.

- Use transitions to show changes in time.

- Use transitions to show how things are alike and how they are different.

- Use transitions to point out causes and results.

Part A   Read the paragraph below. Find seven transitions. List them on your paper.

Shirley
by Derek Corelli

Everyone I know wants to meet Shirley. First there is my mom. At least once a day, she asks me when she will meet Shirley. Then there are my friends, Laura and Amanda. Lately all they talk about is Shirley. Finally, there is my best friend, Mike, who keeps asking, "When, Derek, when?" At last their lucky day is almost here! Tomorrow, at the last track meet of the year, they will all meet Shirley.

Part B   Practice using transitions. Write a paragraph about a recent event in your town or city. Include at least three of the transitions from the lists on page 208. Remember to use sentence variety, too!

Comparison

A statement about how two or more things are alike or different.

Whenever you tell how things are alike or different, you are making a **comparison**. When you write, you often **compare** people, places, things, or ideas.

The sentences below all show common ways to make comparisons.

Compare

To point out ways in which two or more things are alike or different.

EXAMPLES   Shirley is as tall as Laura.

Shirley's hair is shorter than Amanda's.

Shirley's time for the mile is the best on the team.

You can also use less common comparisons to add interest to your sentences. Notice the bold comparisons in Derek's sentences below.

Why I Run
by Derek Corelli

I feel **as if I'm flying**.
The track **is made of sky**.
I am **like a bird**.
My legs are **as strong as an eagle's wings**.

Activity A   On your paper write an ending to each of the comparisons below. Use your imagination.

1) A day without ice cream is like

2) The lake was as clear as

3) A book is like a

4) Before the tournament, Derek was as nervous as

5) The cat's purring sounded like

6) The elephant looked as big as

7) My computer is like

Direct and Indirect Comparisons

Direct comparison

An expression showing that two things have similar qualities; also called a **metaphor**.

You may want to use a **direct comparison** to help your readers form a sharp, interesting picture. A direct comparison is also called a **metaphor**.

EXAMPLE	**Direct Comparison**
	When she runs, Shirley is a deer.
	(Shirley is directly compared to a deer. The reader can picture a fast, graceful runner.)

Indirect comparison

An expression using like *or as to show that two things are like each other in a certain way; also called a* **simile**.

You may also point out how different things are alike with an **indirect comparison**. An indirect comparison uses *like* or *as*. An indirect comparison is also called a **simile**.

EXAMPLES	**Indirect Comparisons**
	Shirley runs like a deer.
	When she is in a race, Shirley is as fierce as a tiger.

Activity B Each of the sentences below contains a comparison. The comparison is a familiar saying. Decide whether the comparison is direct or indirect. Write *Direct* or *Indirect* as your answer. Be ready to discuss the meaning of each familiar saying.

1) The woman is a puzzle to me.

2) The man eats like a horse.

3) That sentence is as clear as mud.

4) Shirley is a breath of fresh air.

5) Shirley is as sweet as honey!

Activity C   Now try to make indirect and direct comparisons that are NOT familiar sayings. Rewrite each sentence below. Include an interesting comparison in it.

1) When I stood before the audience, I felt nervous.
2) Derek talks about Shirley constantly.
3) Basketball players are tall.
4) The TV announcer spoke fast.
5) Laura has a beautiful singing voice.

Exaggerations

Exaggerate

To overstate; to say that something is greater than it is.

When you **exaggerate**, you say that something is greater than it is. An exaggeration is a comparison that helps readers understand your feelings. An exaggeration can entertain your readers. Notice the exaggerations in each of these sentences.

EXAMPLES   Shirley is the most beautiful girl that ever lived.

Your smile is brighter than any star in the sky!

When the roller coaster reached the top of the first hill, I looked down. The bottom was at least one thousand feet below me!

Activity D   Complete the following statements on your paper. Write a beginning for each exaggeration.

Example   . . . more honest than George Washington.

How could I lie? I've always been more honest than George Washington.

1)   . . . worth a million dollars to me.

2)   . . . flew as high as an astronaut.

3)   . . . more frightened than a mouse.

4)   . . . like a sudden clap of thunder.

5)   . . . as tall as a tree.

6)   . . . blew up like a volcano!

Activity E   Write a sentence that describes each of the items below. Include a comparison that exaggerates.

Example   The most boring person you have ever met
Spending the day with him was like spending a day watching the hands move around a clock.

1) The tallest building that you have ever seen

2) The most delicious dessert that you have ever eaten

3) The most difficult task that you have ever completed

4) The most exciting day of your life

5) The most beautiful song that you have ever heard

6) The most energetic child that you have ever met

7) The worst meal that you have ever tasted

8) The proudest moment that you have ever experienced

9) A behavior that annoys you

10) An experience that you would never want to have again

Use comparisons to show how two or more things are alike or different. Use imaginative comparisons such as exaggerations to make your ideas clear and lively.

Part A Match each sentence beginning at the left with a sentence ending at the right. Write the completed sentence on your paper. Be ready to explain what each comparison means.

Column 1

I was so nervous that my hands

Snowflakes were

An unexpected compliment

Riding in Mike's old car

We settled down as happily as

Column 2

as large as cotton balls.

was like being inside a bouncing ball.

chicks in a nest.

is like a rainbow appearing suddenly overhead.

fluttered like frightened butterflies with no safe place to land.

Part B Write five sentences that compare someone you like to other people or things. Exaggerate if you wish.

Part A   Each topic sentence below needs improvement. Rewrite it so that it grabs a reader's attention.

1) This paragraph will be about eating healthy foods.

2) Some kinds of music are great.

3) I think it would be good to have a job in the medical field.

4) Let me tell you about an interesting experience.

5) I am going to write about the history of our town.

6) A dictionary is a useful book.

7) Do you know what I saw last week?

Part B   Three paragraphs follow. They all need improvement. Read each paragraph. Then think about how to make it more interesting to read. Vary the sentence beginnings. Add adjectives, adverbs, or prepositional phrases. Combine some of the ideas into longer sentences. Use transitions to make clear connections. Write the improved paragraph on your paper.

1)

My Retirement
by Derek Corelli

Mike and I played in several tennis tournaments. We lost the first ones. We did improve. We found really bad tennis players. We won our last tournament. We even got a trophy. It was over. I decided not to play again. I am just too busy for tennis.

2)

The Grand Canyon

Have you ever seen the Grand Canyon? The canyon is a national park in Arizona. Thousands of people visit it. The people come mainly in the summer. The Colorado River formed this canyon. The canyon is 277 miles long. It is 4 to 14 miles wide at the rim. It is the most spectacular canyon in the United States.

3)

> **The Right Amount of Sleep**
>
> How much sleep does a person need? Some people need ten hours a night. Some people need only four. Figure out how much sleep you need. Choose three days when you don't need to get up at a particular time. Go to bed at the same time each of those three nights. Notice what time you wake up in the morning. By the third morning, you should know how much sleep your body needs.

Part C Read each sentence below. Notice the common comparison that is in it. Think about the meaning of the sentence. Rewrite the sentence to include a different comparison. Try to make your comparison lively.

1) Mike is as strong as an ox.

2) Derek looks like a million bucks today!

3) The math problem is as clear as mud.

4) That house is as old as the hills.

5) Passing the test was as easy as pie.

Test Taking Tip When studying for a test, write your own test problems with a partner. Then complete each other's test. Double-check your answers.

Chapter

10

Answering Questions

How do you feel about taking tests? If you're like most students, you would rather be doing something else. Tests may never be fun, but there are ways to make them easier to take. The most important thing to do is to prepare. You will feel more sure of yourself if you have studied well.

You can also improve your test scores if you learn how to answer questions properly. Some test questions require short answers, usually complete sentences. Some test questions require longer answers—one or more paragraphs.

In Chapter 10, you will learn how to give written answers to test questions.

Goals for Learning

▶ To answer test questions in complete sentences
▶ To write answers to essay test questions in well-organized paragraphs

Use a complete sentence to answer a test question. Remember that a complete sentence expresses a complete idea. It must include both a subject and a predicate. Study the sample short answers to the questions below.

EXAMPLES

Question: Who was William Bradford?

Answer: William Bradford was a Pilgrim and the second governor of Plymouth Colony.

Question: What unusual geologic features can be found in Yellowstone National Park?

Answer: Yellowstone National Park is famous for its numerous geysers and hot springs.

Activity A   Write one or two sentences to answer each of the questions below. You may use a reference book. The answers can be found in a dictionary, an encyclopedia, or an almanac. Be sure that your answers are in complete sentences.

1) Why is Galileo famous?

2) Who was Frederick Douglass?

3) Why are pictures of Cupid often included on valentines?

4) Where is Denali National Park?

5) What is a Nobel Prize?

6) Where is Pearl Harbor?

7) What is the capital of Colorado?

8) What did Marie Curie accomplish?

9) At what temperature on the Fahrenheit scale will water boil?

10) What is a caterpillar?

11) Describe a Persian cat.

12) What does the word *proficient* mean?

Identify

To tell the most important characteristics of something; these characteristics make the person, place, or thing different or recognizable.

Identifications

Test items may ask you to **identify** certain people, places, or things. Your answer should state the most important characteristics of the person, place, or thing. Ask yourself, "What makes this person famous? What is unusual about this place? What are the special characteristics of this thing?"

Both sentences below are answers to the same test item. Do you see why the second answer is stronger?

EXAMPLES

Test item: Identify Mammoth Cave.

Poor answer: Mammoth Cave is a big cave that has many visitors.

Better answer: Mammoth Cave is a national park in Kentucky; it has 336 miles of underground passages.

Activity B Identify each of the following. You can find information in this book by looking on the page given in parentheses. Write your answers in complete sentences.

1) St. Paul (page 196)

2) Othello (page 182)

3) *Who's Who* (page 183)

Activity C Choose five of the people listed below. Identify these people in complete sentences. You can find information in a reference book.

- Sandra Day O'Connor
- Rosa Parks
- Robert E. Lee
- Joe Louis
- Jim Thorpe
- Nelson Mandela
- Robin Hood
- Florence Nightingale
- Edgar Allan Poe
- I. M. Pei

When a test item requires short answers, write your answers in complete sentences.

Part A   Read each question and the answer below. Decide if the answer is a complete sentence. Write *Yes* or *No* for each answer.

1) How many rooms are in your home?
Three bedrooms, a living room, dining room, and kitchen.

2) Why is there a picture of Cupid on many valentines?
Because Cupid was the god of love in Roman mythology.

3) Identify Zachary Taylor.
Zachary Taylor was an American general and the twelfth president of the United States.

4) Identify Annapolis.
Annapolis is the capital of the state of Maryland.

5) What is a llama?
A llama is a domesticated animal used in the Andes as a beast of burden and as a source of wool.

Part B   Identify the following items. Write each answer in a complete sentence. Use a reference book if necessary.

1) What is a capybara?

2) Identify Austin, Texas.

3) Identify Francis Scott Key.

4) Identify Eleanor Roosevelt.

5) Identify Glacier National Park.

Essay

A short piece of writing about a single subject or topic.

The directions in an **essay** question usually begin with a word such as *describe, compare, explain,* or *discuss.* An essay answer is one or more paragraphs. To write an essay answer, organize your information well. Start with a topic sentence that states the main idea of your essay. Include your information in the body. End with a summary or conclusion.

Make sure that your topic sentence clearly identifies the subject of your essay. Avoid the vague pronoun *it* or a vague reference to the subject. Study this example.

EXAMPLE

Test item:	What qualities made George Washington a great leader?
Poor topic sentence:	This person had many great qualities.
Better topic sentence:	George Washington showed many qualities of leadership.

Activity A   Read each test item below. Choose the better topic sentence in each case. Write the letter of each answer on your paper.

1) Describe Glacier National Park.
   a) It is a large park in northern Montana.
   b) Glacier National Park is in northern Montana.

2) Discuss the activities people do in the spring.
   a) It is a season for doing things outdoors.
   b) Spring is a season for doing things outdoors.

3) Discuss the advantages and disadvantages of having a garden.
   a) Having a garden involves some advantages and disadvantages.
   b) Here are some good and bad things.

4) Compare a short answer and an essay answer.
   a) One is shorter, and the other has more details.
   b) The main difference between a short answer and an essay answer is the amount of detail.

Activity B Read the question below. Then read each of the three topic sentences. Decide which topic sentence is best. Write the reason for your choice.

Question: How do people in the United States celebrate Valentine's Day?

Topic sentences:

a) There are many ways to celebrate this day.

b) Valentine's Day is celebrated in many ways.

c) It is a day for giving cards and having parties.

Activity C Write a one-paragraph essay about the different ways in which people celebrate Valentine's Day. Use the best topic sentence from Activity B, or write one of your own. Include the details of your answer in the body of your paragraph. End your paragraph with a conclusion or a summary.

Descriptions

Sometimes an essay question will ask you to describe a topic. *To describe* means "to tell about" or "to make a picture with words."

Read the sample description below. The details help readers picture the place.

EXAMPLE

Test item: Describe the Grand Canyon.

Description: The Grand Canyon is an extremely deep gorge of the Colorado River. The Grand Canyon is 277 miles long. It is from four to eighteen miles wide. It is one mile deep. This spectacular canyon in Arizona is a national park. Every year, thousands of visitors come to the Grand Canyon. They stand at the rims and gasp at the vast scene before them.

Activity D   Write a paragraph to describe each place below. Include facts about each item that will help your readers picture it.

1) Your house or apartment

2) Your school or your classroom

3) A park in your town or city

Discussions

Sometimes an essay test item will ask you to discuss a topic. To **discuss,** tell about what is good and what is bad about the topic. A discussion often includes opinions. Study the example.

EXAMPLE

Test item: Discuss jogging.

Discussion answer:

To *jog* means "to run slowly." Usually, jogging is good exercise. Because it is an aerobic exercise, jogging stimulates the heart and lungs. Still, doctors recommend that joggers get physical checkups before beginning an exercise program. Jogging is a cheap and easily available form of exercise. No special equipment, other than proper shoes, is needed. Although jogging can be done year-round, it is not so enjoyable in hot, cold, or stormy weather. However, because of its numerous benefits, many people are jogging to improve their physical fitness.

Activity E   Choose one of the topics below. Think of a smaller topic within it. (For example, if you choose *Television*, think about one kind of program or a particular program.) Write at least one paragraph about this topic. Remember to include both good and bad characteristics of this topic.

- Television
- Movies
- Music
- Sports
- Vacations
- Education

Read Carefully!

Always be sure to read the essay question carefully. Follow the exact directions. Even if an answer contains correct information, it will be marked wrong if it does not answer the specific test question.

Activity F Read each of the test items and answers below. None of the answers is correct. Give a reason why each answer below would be marked wrong. Write your reasons in complete sentences.

1) Tell how Valentine's Day was celebrated long ago.

> Valentine's Day in the United States is celebrated by sending cards. These cards often ask the person to "Be My Valentine." Someone's valentine is a special friend. People usually enjoy receiving valentines.

2) Discuss the achievements of Millard Fillmore.

> Millard Fillmore was the thirteenth president of the United States. He became president after Zachary Taylor died in office. Fillmore had been the vice president. He was not reelected to a second term.

3) Describe the Grand Canyon.

> Many people visit the Grand Canyon every year. They sometimes walk on the trails all the way to the bottom of the canyon. It is a very beautiful place. In the summer, the Grand Canyon is very crowded.

4) Why do many people plant vegetable gardens?

> Planting a vegetable garden is becoming more popular every year. In a small area, people can grow vegetables as well as flowers. Even people in apartments often have a small garden. Tomatoes can be grown in flower pots on a balcony.

An essay is a piece of writing about a single subject or topic. An essay answer is made up of one or several paragraphs. Remember these points when you answer an essay test item:

- Read the question carefully.

- Be sure that your first sentence clearly identifies the subject of the essay.

- Be sure that your essay specifically answers the question asked.

Part A Choose one of the topics listed below. Write an essay answer on your paper.

- Discuss a popular musician.

- Describe a house you would like to own someday.

- Tell about an unusual animal.

- Explain why summer is a busy time of year.

Part B Proofread, revise, and rewrite your essay. Refer to the checklist on page 185. Check spelling, punctuation, capitalization, sentence variety, and verb tense.

Chapter 10 Review

Part A   Answer these questions in complete sentences.

1) What is your favorite dessert?

2) Where do you like to go for a vacation?

3) What time do you usually get to school?

4) What kind of music do you like best?

5) Who teaches your English class?

6) Who is a sports star today?

7) Who is the author of a book you have read recently?

8) Who is a government leader in the news?

9) Where is the public library nearest your home?

10) What job or career seems interesting to you?

Part B   Use a reference source to find the answer to each question below. Write each answer in one or two complete sentences.

1) Where is Acadia National Park?

2) What did Thomas Edison invent?

3) When did astronauts first land on the moon?

4) Who was the first woman to win a Nobel Prize in science?

5) How far is Hawaii from San Francisco, California?

6) What is a kudu?

7) Who is Toni Morrison?

8) Where is Palau?

9) When did William Shakespeare write his plays?

10) Where is the Zuñi Pueblo located?

Part C   Read each test item. Then read the topic sentence that follows. The topic sentence is supposed to lead into the rest of the essay. If you think the topic sentence is a good one, write *Correct*. If the topic sentence is poor, rewrite it to make it better.

1) Discuss the use of fuel oil as an energy source.
   Fuel oil is a source of energy that has advantages and disadvantages.

2) Describe the planet Mars.
   It is a planet that is close to Earth.

3) Tell about the first moon landing.
   This was an event that amazed everyone.

4) Explain the origin of Mother's Day.
   The American holiday of Mother's Day was suggested by a woman in Philadelphia.

5) What qualities did Thomas Edison have that made him successful?
   Thomas Edison was a famous inventor.

Part D   Choose one of the topics below. Write a one-paragraph essay on the topic. Remember to start your essay with a topic sentence.

- Tell about the characteristics of an ideal friend.

- Describe your favorite vacation place.

- Give a brief history of an American holiday.

- Discuss an Olympic sport.

Test Taking Tip   When you read over your written answer, imagine that you are someone reading it for the first time. Ask yourself if the ideas and information make sense. Revise and rewrite to make the answer as clear as you can.

Chapter

11

Messages and Memorandums

I magine this situation. You are waiting at the entrance to a store. You had told your friend to meet you there at three o'clock. It is now three-thirty. Where is your friend? You are worried. Why hasn't your friend arrived? You are also annoyed. "How much longer should I wait?" you ask yourself.

When these mixups occur, the cause is often a missed communication. Maybe your friend left a message for you, but you never got it. Maybe you forgot to tell your friend exactly where to meet you. Missed or confused communications can cause all sorts of problems.

In Chapter 11, you will learn one way to avoid missed communications. You will learn how to write clear, complete messages.

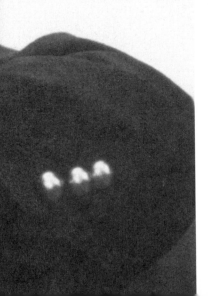

Goals for Learning

▶ To write clear messages
▶ To include all necessary information in messages and memorandums

Message

Communication,
either written
or spoken.

A **message** is any kind of communication. Friends and family members often leave messages to inform one another of plans. Taking messages is an important job in many offices.

Messages may be spoken or written. A written message is more often handwritten than typed. Be careful to make your handwriting readable. Also be sure to include all necessary information.

This list shows the main elements to include in any message:

- The time and date that you wrote the message
- The name of the person who told you the information
- The information needed by the person who gets the message
- Your name, to show who wrote the message

Read the message below. It is written completely and correctly. The person receiving the message has been given all the information she needs to know.

> 3:00 P.M. Monday
>
> Laura,
>
> Amanda called at 3:00 P.M. Call her at home if you get home before 4:30. She'll be at her dancing class until 5:30. Then she'll be home.
>
> Love,
> Mom

Activity A   Use the message above to answer the following questions. Write your answers on your paper.

1) What time did Amanda call?

2) Who took this message?

3) Who is to get this message?

4) What is Laura supposed to do?

5) It is now 5:00 P.M. Is Amanda home?

Activity B   Read each message below. Decide what important information has been left out. Write the missing information on your paper.

Mom, I'm going out. I'll be home later.
Amanda

Laura, Derek called. Call him back.
Mom

MIKE, YOU ARE SUPPOSED TO PLAY TENNIS.   TIM

Dad, someone called about the car.

Mr. Martin, I stopped by during second period to ask about my homework. I'll be back.
Amanda

Ms. Lawson, I NEED AN APPOINTMENT TO TALK TO YOU. I'LL BE BACK AT THREE O'CLOCK.

Activity C   Imagine that you have answered the phone at home. You need to write a message for a family member. List at least five kinds of information that you would want to include in such a message.

When you take a message, remember to include all necessary information. In addition to the message itself, include the time and date, the name of the caller, and your name. Remember to write neatly, too.

Part A Write a message to a member of your family. Explain that you went to the store and will be home in time for dinner. Include these five elements in your message.

1) Date
2) Time
3) Name of person who is receiving the message
4) Message
5) Your name

Part B Read the telephone dialogue below. Then write the message that Derek should write for Coach Jones. Include all necessary information. Use today's date.

Derek is walking past the coach's office at 2:30 P.M. The telephone rings. He answers it.

Derek: Hello. This is the Springfield Physical Education Department. The coach isn't here. May I help you?

Woman: Yes, this is the Springfield Sporting Goods Company. Coach Jones ordered ten baseball bats.

Derek: Yes. What should I tell him?

Woman: Tell him that the bats are ready. He can pick them up anytime between 9 A.M. and 6 P.M. except on Sunday.

Derek: Who should I say called?

Woman: My name is Ms. Handley. If he has any questions, he can call me at 577-8900.

Derek: OK. I've got the message.

Woman: Thank you. Good-bye.

Memorandum

An informal message written in special form and frequently used in the business world; often shortened to memo.

A **memorandum** is often called by its shorter name—*memo*. A memo is a special kind of written message. It seems like a letter, but it is less formal. Unlike a letter, a memo is not usually sent by mail. Instead, a memo may be delivered to the employees of a company. Memos are common in business settings.

Read the sample memo below. It gives brief information about an event.

MEMO

Date: May 3, 20–
To: Ms. Hall
From: Ms. Lawson, Chairperson, Awards Committee   *ACL*
Subject: Awards Assembly

   The Awards Assembly will be held on Monday, June 10, at 2:00 P.M. Because of lack of space in the auditorium, the committee decided that only the seniors would be invited to attend. If these plans are all right, please let me know.

   The next meeting of the Awards Committee will be held on May 12 at 3:30 P.M. in room 216. We will discuss the decoration of the stage and the program for the assembly.

Activity A   Write the answers to these questions. Use the information in the sample memo above.

1) What four words are printed on most memo forms?

2) There is no address included on this memo. Why not?

3) Does the writer sign his or her name on a memo?

4) What did the committee decide?

5) What will happen on Monday, June 10, at 2:00 P.M.?

6) What will happen on May 12 at 3:30 P.M.?

7) In what room will the meeting be held?

8) What will be discussed at this meeting?

9) Who sent this memo? Who received it?

10) After reading the memo above, what would you say is the purpose of a memo?

Activity B   Practice writing a memo. Start by writing the heading *Memo* at the top of a sheet of paper. Then take the following steps.

1) List these words: *Date, To, From,* and *Subject.*

2) Put a colon (:) after each of the listed words.

3) Choose one of the topics below.

4) Write a memo. Give all necessary information.

- Write a memo to a parent. Make a request for something you need.
- Write a memo to your teacher. Explain why you should not have homework on the weekend.
- Write a memo to someone in your class. Ask to borrow a computer game.

Activity C   Read the message below. Rewrite it in memo form. Include all necessary information. Use today's date.

Dear Coach Jones,

Several weeks ago you spoke to me about ordering ten new baseball bats from the Springfield Sporting Goods Company.

Have these new bats arrived? Will ten bats be sufficient for both the boys' and girls' teams?

Please give me the bill for the bats when they arrive. I will see that it is paid promptly.

Sincerely,

Ms. B. Hall,
Principal

A memo is a message written in a special form. Memos are common in business settings. Memos must include all necessary information.

Part A Read the memo below. Then answer the questions that follow.

MEMO

Date: May 7, 20–
To: Ms. Hall
From: Coach Jones *HMJ*
Subject:

    I have attached to this memo the bill for the ten new baseball bats. The boys' team has a sufficient number of bats. These ten new baseball bats are for the girls' team. This year is the first year for the girls' team, we needed these bats to complete our stock of new equipment.

---

1) What information is missing from this memo?

2) Should Coach Jones have signed his name?

3) Why is an address not included on this memo?

4) What is the sentence error? Correct it on your paper.

Part B Read the message below. Rewrite it in memo form. Include all necessary information. Use today's date.

Dear Coach,

    We have paid the bill for the new baseball bats from the Springfield Sporting Goods Company Thank you for ordering this equipment for the girls' team.

                Sincerely,

                Ms. B. Hall
                Principal

Part A   Read the following conversation between Derek and his mother. Write the message that is to be given to Shirley. Use complete sentences.

Derek:	It is nearly three o'clock. I have to go to work. Tell Shirley that I'll be home by six. I'll meet her at school.
Ms. Corelli:	You'll have to eat dinner before you go out.
Derek:	OK. Tell her I'll meet her at seven.
Ms. Corelli:	I'll give her your message.

Part B   Imagine that you are baby-sitting for little Tanya at the Jefferson home this evening. You answer the telephone and explain that Ms. Jefferson has gone out for the evening. This is the information the caller gives you:

- "My name is Denise Stith."
- "I am Tanya Jefferson's aunt."
- "I cannot meet Ms. Jefferson tomorrow evening."
- "I will try to call Ms. Jefferson tomorrow."
- "Tell Ms. Jefferson I'm sorry about the change in plans."

Use the information to write a message for Ms. Jefferson, Tanya's mother. Include all necessary information.

Part C   Copy the parts of the memo below onto your paper. Write a message to your teacher, a friend, or a family member. Choose any subject you wish. Include all necessary information. Use today's date.

MEMO

Date:
To:
From:
Subject:

Part D Rewrite the message below. Put it into memo form. Use today's date.

11:00 A.M., Tuesday

Luis,

　　The chess club is meeting in room 111 tomorrow. Mr. Harris says he has an important announcement. Try to come early, before three o'clock.

　　　　　　　　　　　　　　　　Mia

Part E Find five errors in the following memo. List them on your paper.

MEMO

Date: April 3, 20–
To: Mr. Henry Tso
Subject: Vacation days

　　I have received your request to take five days of vacation from Monday, June 12, through Friday, June 16, the request has been approved. I hope you have a great time in arizona!

　　　　　　　　　　　　Best wishes,

　　　　　　　　　　　　Fred Lamont

Test Taking Tip When you read test directions, try to restate them in your own words. Tell yourself what you are expected to do. That way, you can make sure your answer will be complete and correct.

Writing Letters

Have you ever written a thank-you note for a gift? Have you ever received a long letter from a family member far away? Have you ever written a letter to a complete stranger? What are some other kinds of letters you can think of?

Whether you write a personal letter or a business letter, remember to express your ideas clearly. Use correct sentences and well-organized paragraphs, and your reader will appreciate your message.

Chapter 12 discusses several purposes and kinds of personal letters. You will also learn two standard styles for business letters.

Goals for Learning

▶ To know the parts of a letter

▶ To write business and personal letters

▶ To address an envelope

Personal letter

An informal message written to a friend or a relative.

When you write a **personal letter**, you share news and feelings with a friend or family member. A personal letter is also called a friendly letter. It has a simple five-part format. Study the five parts of the personal letter below.

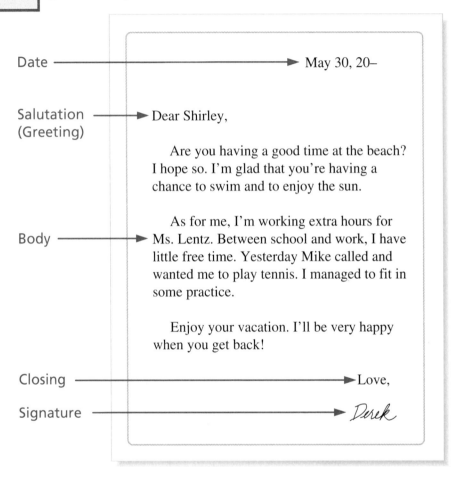

Date ———————————————▶ May 30, 20–

Salutation ———▶ Dear Shirley,
(Greeting)

     Are you having a good time at the beach? I hope so. I'm glad that you're having a chance to swim and to enjoy the sun.

Body ———————▶   As for me, I'm working extra hours for Ms. Lentz. Between school and work, I have little free time. Yesterday Mike called and wanted me to play tennis. I managed to fit in some practice.

     Enjoy your vacation. I'll be very happy when you get back!

Closing ———————————————▶ Love,

Signature ———————————————▶ *Derek*

Activity A   Use the sample letter above to answer these questions.

1) What mark of punctuation follows the salutation?

2) What closing does Derek use in this letter?

3) What mark of punctuation follows the closing?

4) Which part of a letter contains the message?

5) What part of a letter is also called the greeting?

Invitations

You may write a friendly letter to invite someone to join you at an event. An invitation should include all necessary facts:

> - Description of the event
> - Details about when and where the event is taking place
> - Transportation, prices, special clothing, and so on

The sample letter below includes all necessary details. As you read the letter, look for the details.

May 18, 20–

Dear Joan,

Hi! I've got wonderful news. John and I were able to rent the cabin at the lake for two weeks in July. There is plenty of room for your family and ours, so we hope that you can join us as our guests. The children will have a wonderful time.

The cabin is furnished, including linens, pots and pans, and dishes. I'll send you a map with directions to the cabin. All that is needed for a great time is for our two families to be there!

The exact dates are from July 6 to July 20. If you can arrange to be there, please write me as soon as possible. Isn't this a tricky way to get a letter from you?

Michelle

Activity B   Write an invitation to someone you know. Choose one of the topics below. Use the five-part format shown in this lesson. Include all necessary information: event, location, time, date, cost, and so on. Remember to write neatly!

- An invitation to a sporting event
- An invitation to a party
- An invitation to a movie, a play, or a concert
- An invitation to a school event that will be held soon
- An invitation to your teacher to attend a school or community event in which you are participating

Thank-You Letters

It is always polite to say thank you for a gift or a favor. It is even more thoughtful to say it in a letter. Read the sample letter below. Notice that the writer has described the gift in detail. Such personal comments show that the gift was truly appreciated.

August 6, 20—

Dear Aunt Marie,

I want to thank you for the wonderful soft sweater that you sent. It was so thoughtful of you to remember my birthday. How did you ever guess that the sweater was exactly what I wanted? It fits perfectly. Blue is my favorite color, too.

The rest of the family says hello. I am looking forward to seeing you soon.

Love,

Carolyne

Activity C   Write a thank-you letter to someone who has given you a gift or done a favor for you. Be specific. Make positive comments. (You may want to mail this letter.)

Envelopes

Address your envelope clearly and correctly. Then your letter will arrive on time. Study the information in the sample at the top of the next page.

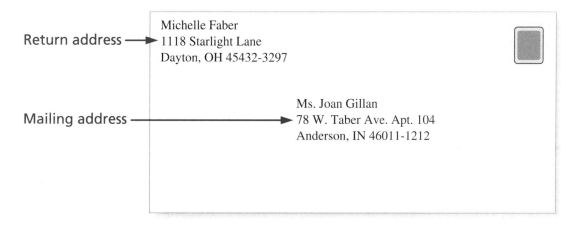

Return address → Michelle Faber
1118 Starlight Lane
Dayton, OH 45432-3297

Mailing address → Ms. Joan Gillan
78 W. Taber Ave. Apt. 104
Anderson, IN 46011-1212

Use the proper abbreviation for the state followed by the ZIP code. Use the complete ZIP+4 code if you know it. Write as clearly as you can. The US Postal Service recommends that if you are writing by hand, print in all capital letters.

Activity D   Write your answer to the following questions in complete sentences. Refer to the sample envelope above.

1) What is a return address?

2) What is a mailing address?

3) What is usually written on the first line of an address?

4) What is usually written on the second line of an address?

5) What is usually written on the third line of an address?

6) What punctuation mark is used between the city and the state?

Activity E   Read the following three sample addresses. Find the error in each one. Rewrite all three addresses correctly on your paper.

1) Thomas, Dottie
4398 First Avenue
Rosedale, MD 20840-3129

2) Carlos Riverez
60 Harris St.
01060-2224 Hampton, MA

3) BETH SIMMINS
HARGATE, TN 37752-4008
RTE 2, BOX 407

Activity F Practice addressing envelopes correctly.

1) Address an envelope to someone you know. Use your address as the return address.

2) Address an envelope to yourself. Use your school address as the return address.

Letters to Keep in Touch

A good reason for writing a personal letter is just to keep in touch with friends and family members. Even everyday events can be of interest to the person who receives your letter.

Here are some topics that you could write about:

- Tell about a book, a movie, a song, or a television program.

- Tell about school. What are you studying? Do you have a report that is due soon? What are your teachers like? Are you active in a program, a team, or a club?

- Tell about something you did that was fun or boring. Tell about something you plan to do.

- Tell about vacations or vacation plans.

- Tell about what has happened in your life since you saw the person.

- Tell about a hobby or a sport.

Activity G Think of a friend or a relative who would like to receive a letter from you. Jot down some of the topics you might tell this person about.

Read this sample letter. Notice that it includes some of the topics suggested on page 246.

May 3, 20–

Dear Richard,

I bet you're surprised to get this letter from me. Well, I had to do a letter for my English class. I decided to write to you because I thought that you might write me back.

School is going well. I'm spending a lot of time in the technology center. I'm getting to be an expert at upgrading personal computer systems. My computer course is my favorite. Guess what else? Only 40 days until graduation! Did you think I could do it?

I've also been busy outside of school. I won a tennis tournament. Lately, I've been playing softball. I had a single and a double last night. I had to slide into second, but I made it! Oh, yes, I'm jogging five miles a day now. Sometimes I jog with Derek.

Write soon.

Your friend,

Mike

Activity H　Look at the topics you listed in Activity G. Think about the friend or relative who will receive your letter. Add any other topic that would interest this person. Write the letter. Follow the form for a personal letter given in this lesson. Include all necessary parts. Write neatly. Address the envelope correctly. Then stamp and mail your letter.

Personal letters are an informal way to share news and feelings with a friend or a relative. When you write a personal letter, remember these points:

- Date your letter.
- Include a salutation or greeting. (Dear Joan,)
- Write your message in the body of the letter.
- Add a closing. (Yours,)
- Sign your name.
- Address the envelope correctly.
- Stamp and mail the letter.

Part A Read this sample thank-you letter. Find three format errors. List the errors on your paper.

Derek

Dear Aunt Harriet

It was so thoughtful of you to remember my birthday. You are so generous! I really needed the money. I need new running shoes for the next track meet. Thanks! Love,

Derek

Part B Write a personal letter to a friend or a relative. It may be an invitation, a thank-you, or just a letter to keep in touch. After your teacher returns the letter to you, put it into an envelope and mail it.

Business letter

A formal message written to a person or an organization.

You may write a **business letter** to request information from an organization. You may also write to discuss a product or service, or to apply for a job. A business letter is more formal than a personal letter.

Here are the other main differences between the two letters:

- Stationery for personal letters comes in many sizes and colors. The standard size for a business letter is $8\frac{1}{2} \times 11$ inches. White or off-white paper is usually preferred for a business letter.

- A personal letter may be handwritten. A business letter should be typed.

- Both sides of the paper may be used for a personal letter. Only one side of the paper is used for a business letter.

- A personal letter has five main parts. A business letter has eight main parts.

Read about the eight parts of a business letter.

1. **The heading, or return address,** gives the address of the sender. Business stationery often has an imprinted heading that includes the company name.

2. **The date** helps businesses keep track of correspondence.

3. **The inside address** shows who is receiving the letter.

4. **The salutation, or greeting,** includes the title and last name of the person being addressed. A colon comes after the salutation. Here are some examples of business letter salutations:
   Dear Dr. Jackson: Dear Sir or Madam: Dear Editor:

5. **The body** contains the message, usually in several paragraphs.

6. **The closing, or complimentary close,** is more formal than the closing in a personal letter. Only the first letter of the first word is capitalized. A closing always ends with a comma. Here are some examples of business letter closings:
   Yours truly,   Sincerely,   Respectfully yours,
   Very truly yours,   Sincerely yours,   Cordially,

7. **The handwritten signature** appears above the typed name.

8. **The typed name and title** appear four lines below the closing.

Activity A   Compare the eight parts of a business letter with the five parts of a personal letter. (See page 242.) What three parts are in a business letter that are *not* in a personal letter? List each part and write a brief description of its purpose.

Study the eight parts of this sample business letter. Notice the two additional parts at the bottom of the letter. They are labeled *Optional notations*. The first notation shows that Lynda Handley did not type her own letter. It was typed by her secretary, Cindy King. The second notation shows that a brochure is included in the envelope with this letter.

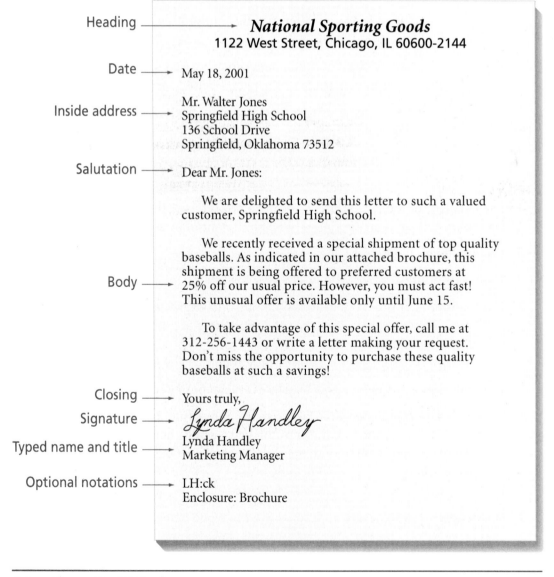

Heading ──────────→ **National Sporting Goods**
1122 West Street, Chicago, IL 60600-2144

Date ──→ May 18, 2001

Inside address ──→ Mr. Walter Jones
Springfield High School
136 School Drive
Springfield, Oklahoma 73512

Salutation ──→ Dear Mr. Jones:

We are delighted to send this letter to such a valued customer, Springfield High School.

We recently received a special shipment of top quality baseballs. As indicated in our attached brochure, this shipment is being offered to preferred customers at
Body ──→ 25% off our usual price. However, you must act fast! This unusual offer is available only until June 15.

To take advantage of this special offer, call me at 312-256-1443 or write a letter making your request. Don't miss the opportunity to purchase these quality baseballs at such a savings!

Closing ──→ Yours truly,

Signature ──→ *Lynda Handley*

Typed name and title ──→ Lynda Handley
Marketing Manager

Optional notations ──→ LH:ck
Enclosure: Brochure

Activity B Write your answers to these questions about the sample letter on page 250.

1) Notice that the heading (the return address) is printed on the stationery in a different type. What part is added just below the heading?

2) Did someone from National Sporting Goods or Springfield High School write this letter? How can you tell?

3) What punctuation mark is used after the salutation?

4) Read the body of the letter. What does Lynda Handley want Coach Jones to do?

5) Give one reason why Coach Jones might want to do this.

6) What closing is used in this letter? What are three other closings that could be used in a business letter?

7) Why is Lynda Handley's name typed on the letter below her signature?

8) What is Lynda Handley's job title?

9) What do the letters *LH:ck* mean? Why are they typed on this business letter?

The sample letter on page 250 is typed in *block style*. Block style is the most formal style. It is often used when the business stationery has a letterhead. All parts of the letter begin at the left margin. The paragraphs are not indented.

Another style to use for business letters is the *modified block style*. Several lines begin near the middle of the page: the return address, the date, the closing, the handwritten signature, and the typed name. All the other parts begin at the left margin. Each paragraph of the body is indented. The sample letter on page 252 is typed in modified block style.

18 Silver Lane
Springfield, OK 73510
May 12, 20–

Mr. Paul Elliott
Western Industries
One Western Plaza
Centerville, Texas 79408

Dear Mr. Elliott:

This letter is in response to your advertisement in the *Daily News.* I would like to apply for the position of ticket agent. I understand that this position is temporary and will last only during the rodeo season.

For the past year, I have been employed at a gas station. My duties included selling parts and using a cash register. I believe I have the experience necessary to be a ticket agent.

I will call you on May 20. You may reach me at 405-234-7766 before then. I am available any Saturday for an interview.

Thank you for considering me for this position.

Sincerely,

Derek Corelli

Derek Corelli

Activity C Refer to the sample letter on page 252. Write your answers to these questions in complete sentences.

1) What punctuation mark is used after the salutation?
2) What punctuation mark is used after the closing?
3) What are the numbers *79408*?
4) How is the style of this letter different from the style of the sample letter on page 250?
5) What is the main purpose of this letter?
6) A business letter should come to the point quickly. Has Derek come to the point quickly? Has he included all necessary information? Explain your answer.

Activity D Choose one of these topics for a business letter.

• Write a letter to a local museum. Request information about an exhibit. Include a reason for wanting this information.

• Write to a local radio or television station. Express your opinion about a program. Include facts to back up your opinion.

• Write to a local business. Ask about summer employment. Include facts about your job experiences, educational background, and personal qualifications. Make the company want to hire you!

• Write a letter to the editor of a local newspaper. Express your opinion about a recent event in your city. Include facts to back up this opinion.

After you have chosen a topic, use the telephone directory to find addresses. Use your own return address. Type or write a business letter. Organize the body of your letter in this way:

1) In paragraph 1, introduce yourself or briefly explain why you are writing the letter.
2) In paragraph 2, request the information or state your opinion. Be specific. What do you want this person or organization to do for you? Include all necessary information.
3) In paragraph 3, express your thanks.

Check your letter to make sure you have included all eight parts correctly.

Mailing a Business Letter

Before you insert your business letter into an envelope, fold it in thirds. Follow these steps:

1. Place the letter face up on the desk.
2. Fold a little less than a third of the sheet from the bottom toward the top and crease.
3. Fold the top third down to one-fourth inch from the first crease.
4. Insert the last fold into the envelope first.

A standard business envelope is $4\frac{1}{8}$ inches by $9\frac{1}{2}$ inches. To prepare a business envelope for mailing, follow these steps:

1. Write or type the complete return address in the top left corner.
2. Write or type the complete mailing address in the center of the envelope, a little to the right.
3. Write or type the person's name first. If you do not know the person's name, you may write the person's title or position.
4. Put the correct postage on the letter.

Activity E Which of these two envelopes is addressed completely and correctly? Explain the reasons for your choice.

Envelope A

D. Diamond
1234 Archmore Rd
Tucson, AZ 85727-2254

Editor
Fashion Flair Magazine
112 Center St
Gainesville, FL 32602-2903

Envelope B

D. Diamond
12324 Archmore Road
Tucson 85727-2254

Fashion Flair Magazine
Della Lyons, Editor
Gainesville, FL 32602-2903
112 Center Street

Activity F Use the business letter you wrote for Activity D. Fold it and insert it into a business envelope. Address the envelope correctly. If you wish, add a stamp and mail your letter.

A business letter is more formal than a personal letter. When you write a business letter, remember to include all eight parts:

- Return address, or heading
- Date
- Inside address
- Salutation, or greeting, followed by a colon
- Body
- Formal closing
- Signature
- Name (and title, if appropriate)

Be clear, correct, and complete when addressing the envelope. The envelope will be the first thing that is noticed. Be sure that it is letter-perfect!

Part A   Read the salutations and closings below. Is each one appropriate for a business letter? Write *Yes* or *No* for each number.

1) Dear Mr. Levin: **5)** Love,

2) Hi, Harry,   **6)** Very truly yours,

3) Dear Manager: **7)** Cordially,

4) To Whom It May Concern: **8)** Take care,

Part B   Write answers to the following items.

1) List the eight parts of a business letter.

2) List two appropriate closings for a business letter.

3) Write the amount of postage that is needed to mail a first-class letter.

4) List three ways in which a business letter is different from a personal letter.

5) Write your complete mailing address.

Part A   Read the following five sample addresses. Each one contains at least one error. Rewrite all five addresses correctly on your paper. (Use your imagination if you need to add information.)

1) Chris Gillan Apt. A
Kentmill Rd.
78
Oakville, PA 15139

2) NORMA STOOPS
1580 ETON WAY
DELRAY BEACH 33445
FLORIDA

3) Mr. Frank Chung
Box 800
Maryland
Annapolis 21401-2218

4) Handy Pencil Company
123 Broadway
Sanford, GA 31402-2435
Eugenia Tillots
Customer Service

5) Student Art Contest
WBTM Radio
Massachusetts 02154-3214

Part B   Write a personal letter to someone who lives near you. Share some news about what you are doing in school. Make sure your letter includes the five basic parts. Then address an envelope. Use your home address as the return address. Use the person's home address as the mailing address. Have your teacher review your letter and envelope. Then add a stamp and mail your letter.

Part C Find the five format errors in the business letter below. List each error on your paper. Show how it could be corrected.

Janine Wittson
421 Dover Street
West Oakley, NY

Ms. Carla Marcos
Consumer Complaint Department
XYZ Greeting Card Company
Claymore, WA 98259

Dear Ms. Marcos,

On September 30, I ordered three boxes of greeting cards: items 1327, 1459, and 2346 from your autumn catalog. I enclosed a check for $43.59, including shipping and handling. I have received the canceled check. Although three months have gone by, I have not received the greeting cards.

I am enclosing a copy of my canceled check and a copy of my order form. I would like to receive the greeting cards as quickly as possible. If they cannot be sent, I would like my money back.

Thank you for your attention to this matter. I look forward to your reply. I can be reached at the address above or by phone at 914-332-6789.

Janine Wittson

Janine Wittson

Enclosures

Part D Write a business letter to anyone you choose. Include the eight main parts. Make sure that your paragraphs are well organized and contain all necessary information. Be sure that your spelling, capitalization, and punctuation are perfect. Refer to the checklist on page 185.

Test Taking Tip When a teacher announces a test, listen carefully. Write down the topics that will be included. Write down the names of any specific readings the teacher says to review.

Chapter

13

Writing a Report

When a teacher assigns a report, do you know how to get the most out of the experience? First of all, try not to think of a report as a difficult chore. Think of it as a chance to learn about something that interests you.

Choose a topic that you are curious about. Track down information. Think about the information. Organize it. Write about it. When you do all those things, you may discover that you have gained valuable understandings.

In Chapter 13, you will learn how to plan and write a report.

Goals for Learning

▶ To make a plan for a report

▶ To find information and take notes

▶ To organize information and make an outline

▶ To write, proofread, revise, and rewrite

▶ To prepare a bibliography

▶ To hand in a good report on time

Report

An organized summary of information about a topic that has been researched; a report may be written or spoken.

Term paper

A formal report in which a writer tries to prove a thesis or an idea about a chosen topic.

Your final goal is to write a well-organized, fact-filled, interesting **report** or **term paper**. Spend some time making a careful plan that will lead you to that final goal. Here are the steps you will follow:

Step 1	Choose a topic.
Step 2	Find information and take notes.
Step 3	Organize your information and make an outline.
Step 4	Write the report; proofread, revise, and rewrite.
Step 5	Prepare the bibliography.
Final Goal	Hand a good report in on time!

Take the first step. Think of topics that interest you. You might start with a subject area and list topics that fall within it. Look at these sample lists.

Science	History	Music
Energy sources	The American Revolution	Popular dances
The atom	Early computers	The orchestra
Earthquakes	Transportation	African music

Activity A Choose one of the subject areas listed below. Then list topics that fall within that subject. List as many topics as you can think of. Finally, circle any topics that you think might be interesting to learn about.

- Science
- History
- Cultures
- Sports

- Geography
- Literature
- Mathematics
- Travel

- Music
- Art
- Technology
- Careers

Suppose that you have chosen the topic *Transportation* within the subject *History*. Here are just some of the questions that could be asked about that topic:

Subject: History
Topic: Transportation

- What were the earliest wheeled vehicles?
- When were motorcycles invented?
- What were the first airplanes like?
- Who invented and improved the automobile?
- What animals have been used in the past for transportation?

You can see that the history of transportation is a broad topic—*too* broad. Try to narrow your topic to one that you can handle in a report. Find **subtopics** within your topic. You may need to find subtopics within your subtopics, too. A report on the history of transportation would be too long and hard to manage. A report on the history of motorcycles, however, may be just the right size.

Subtopic

A division or a part of a larger topic. Video games *is one subtopic under the main topic* Computers, *for example.*

The best topic for a report is neither too broad nor too narrow. If the topic is too broad, there will be too much information to choose from. If the topic is too narrow, you will not find enough information.

Activity B   In each pair below, identify the topic that is broad and the topic that is narrow. Write *Broad* or *Narrow* on your paper.

1) a) Growing vegetables
   b) Growing root vegetables

2) a) Computers from past to present
   b) The first computers

3) a) Schools in the United States
   b) High schools in the United States

4) a) Sun spots
   b) The sun

5) a) The history of Mexico
   b) The Mexican War with the United States

Catalog

A list of items arranged in a special way.

One way to find out whether your topic is too broad or too narrow is to do a quick check at the library. Use the library **catalog** to look up subjects. A library catalog lists every book, magazine, and recording in that library.

The catalog is on a computer in most public libraries. In some libraries, the catalog is still arranged on cards in drawers. In a few libraries, the catalog is on sheets of film called microfiche. Microfiche is read through a special magnifying machine.

Activity C Go to the library catalog to look up each of the subjects below. Write down how many books are available on that subject. Then write whether you think the topic is *Too Broad, Too Narrow,* or *Just Right.*

1) Computers

2) Computers—history

3) Video games

4) Motorcycles

5) Motorcycle racing

6) Solar system

7) Venus—atmosphere

8) Gardening

9) Carrots—gardening

Activity D Look over your own possible report topics. (You listed them in Activity A.) Locate your topics among the subject listings in the library catalog. Decide on the topic you think is best. To decide on your topic, ask yourself these questions:

- Am I truly interested in learning about this topic? (Your answer should be yes.)
- Is the topic too broad? (Narrow it.)
- Is the topic too narrow? (Make it broader.)

Write down the name of your report topic.

You have completed the first step in writing your report:
You have chosen your topic. You may still change your mind,
however. As you work on your report, you may decide to do
any of these things:

- Change your topic completely.
- Make your topic broader.
- Make your topic narrower.

Part A Write your answers to the following questions in
complete sentences.

1) Would *Science* be a good topic for a report? Explain why
   or why not.

2) Why might it be hard to find information on some topics?
   Give two reasons.

3) Why should you check subject records in the library
   catalog *before* you choose a topic?

4) What is an example of a topic that is too broad? What is
   an example of a topic that is too narrow?

5) What is the difference between a main topic and a subtopic?

Part B Each row contains one main topic and three subtopics.
Identify the main topic. Write the main topic on your paper.

1) Vegetables	Turnips	Beans	Carrots
2) Literature	Poetry	Short Stories	Novels
3) Poodles	Dogs	Collies	Terriers
4) Roses	Daisies	Flowers	Marigolds
5) Robins	Crows	Blue Jays	Birds
6) French	Spanish	Languages	English
7) Mars	Venus	Earth	Planets
8) Gardening	Fertilizing	Planting	Weeding
9) Hurdles	Marathon	Long Jump	Olympics
10) Football	Hockey	Sports	Volleyball

Research

To look for information about a topic by reading books and periodicals, by observing events, or by questioning experts.

You have chosen a topic. Now you are ready to find information, or **research** your topic. You will need to keep track of your sources. You will need to take notes as you **investigate** your topic. Where should you begin?

The library catalog is always the best place to begin. If your library has a card catalog, you will find three kinds of cards: title, author, and subject.

Investigate

To search thoroughly; to examine.

- If you know the author's name, look for an author card. It is filed alphabetically by last name. *(Patent, Dorothy Hinshaw)*

- If you know the book title, look for a title card. It is filed alphabetically by the first important word (not *A, An,* or *The*).

- For research, subject cards are probably most useful. Look for a subject card filed alphabetically by the first important word of your topic. If your subject is a person, look for the last name first *(Lincoln, Abraham)*.

The drawers of a card catalog have guide letters on them. The letters show which alphabetized cards are in each drawer. This sample shows six drawers from a card catalog.

A - Am   An - Bo   Br - Ce   Ch - Cy   Da - Ez   Fa - Fy

Activity A   Notice the guide letters on the six drawers above. Write the letters of the drawer containing cards on each subject below.

1) Canyons

2) Ants

3) Earthquakes

4) Dinosaurs

5) Chemistry

6) Agriculture

7) Business

8) Frederick Douglass

Each of the three kinds of cards in the card catalog has the same information. The arrangement is slightly different. Here are three sample cards:

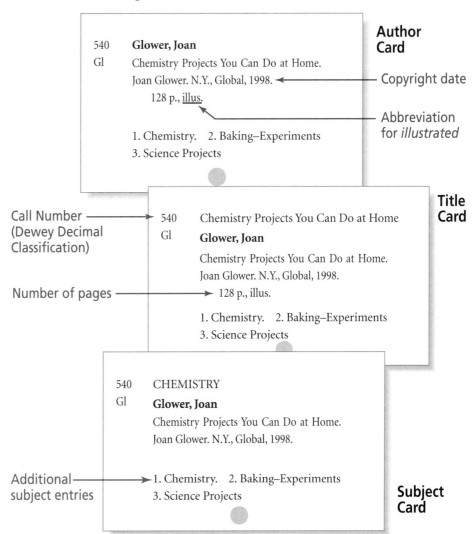

Author Card

540
Gl   **Glower, Joan**
         Chemistry Projects You Can Do at Home.
         Joan Glower. N.Y., Global, 1998. ◄——— Copyright date
            128 p., <u>illus.</u>

                                                    Abbreviation
                                                    for *illustrated*

         1. Chemistry.   2. Baking–Experiments
         3. Science Projects

Title Card

Call Number ——————► 540   Chemistry Projects You Can Do at Home
(Dewey Decimal   Gl   **Glower, Joan**
Classification)   Chemistry Projects You Can Do at Home.
                                 Joan Glower. N.Y., Global, 1998.
Number of pages ——————►   128 p., illus.

                                 1. Chemistry.   2. Baking–Experiments
                                 3. Science Projects

Subject Card

540   CHEMISTRY
Gl   **Glower, Joan**
         Chemistry Projects You Can Do at Home.
         Joan Glower. N.Y., Global, 1998.

Additional ——————►1. Chemistry.   2. Baking–Experiments
subject entries   3. Science Projects

Activity B   Study the information in the sample cards above. Write your answers to the following questions.

1) Why is it important to write down the call number of a book you will look for on the library shelves?
2) In what year was the book by Joan Glower published?
3) What subject did a researcher look for to find this card?
4) Does this book have chemistry projects involving foods? Explain your answer.

Most libraries have computer catalogs. Instructions appear on the screen to tell you what steps to take. You can pull up a listing by typing the author's name, the title, or the subject.

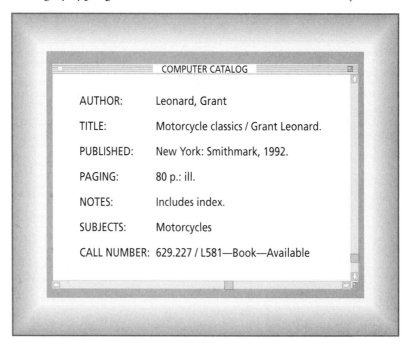

COMPUTER CATALOG

AUTHOR: Leonard, Grant

TITLE: Motorcycle classics / Grant Leonard.

PUBLISHED: New York: Smithmark, 1992.

PAGING: 80 p.: ill.

NOTES: Includes index.

SUBJECTS: Motorcycles

CALL NUMBER: 629.227 / L581—Book—Available

Activity C Study the information in the computer catalog entry above. Write your answers to the following questions.

1) What is the last name of the author of this book?
2) What is the title of this book?
3) How can you tell that this book has pictures in it?
4) Why would the copyright date of a book be important to a researcher?

Activity D Read about each situation below. Write what you would look up in the library catalog.

1) You are writing a report about Albert Einstein.
2) You would like to look at science books written by Patricia Lauber.
3) You are looking for books about motorcycles.
4) You are looking for books about the exploration of Antarctica.
5) You are looking for a book about bulldogs.
6) You would like to find a book about Chinese history called *The Long March.*

Inside Books

The library catalog has led you to a book that might be useful to you. You have used the call number to find the book on the shelf. Now, how can you tell whether the book contains the information you need? Look inside.

The **table of contents** is in the front of the book. It gives you a general sense of the information inside. This is part of a table of contents from a book about transportation.

Contents

The **index** gives more detail about information in the book. The index entry on the left is from the same book about transportation.

Activity E Use the samples on this page to answer the following questions. Write your answers on your paper.

1) On which page of the book about transportation would you find information about how fast ocean liners travel?

2) Which chapter of the book tells about submarines?

3) On which page does the chapter about submarines begin?

4) If your research topic is motorcycles, would this book be useful to you? Why or why not?

5) What other topic could you look up in the index to find out about ocean transportation?

Reference Books

The library catalog lists all books, including those in the reference section of the library. There are many kinds of reference books on all sorts of subjects. Generally, reference books cannot be checked out.

An almanac is published every year. Almanacs contain facts, statistics, and records for current and past years. Major topics covered include sports, inventions, states and nations, and current issues in the news.

An encyclopedia has many volumes. Encyclopedia articles cover a huge range of topics. Use an encyclopedia to get general information on your topic.

An atlas is a book of maps. Atlases also contain facts about cities, states, countries, and world regions.

A biographical dictionary contains information about famous people. Examples are *The International Who's Who* or *Who Was Who in America.*

Activity F Read each question below. Write in which reference book you would find information on that topic: *almanac, atlas, encyclopedia, biographical dictionary.* (There may be more than one correct answer.)

1) Who is the mayor of El Paso, Texas?

2) What major highways cross Montana?

3) How many people visit the Grand Canyon each year?

4) What climates are in Australia?

5) Who was Albert Einstein?

6) What were the first computers like?

7) How should tomatoes be planted?

8) On what day will New Year's Day fall in the year 2050?

9) Where is Malaysia?

10) What plays did Lorraine Hansberry write?

Periodicals

Periodicals

Any printed materials published at regular intervals; magazines and newspapers.

As you research, look for information in magazines and newspapers. Librarians can help you find articles in current and back issues of **periodicals**.

First find out what articles you need. Computer catalogs often contain records for periodicals. Suppose you are researching the history of the Olympic Games. Here is a record from a computer catalog that appears for the subject *Olympics*.

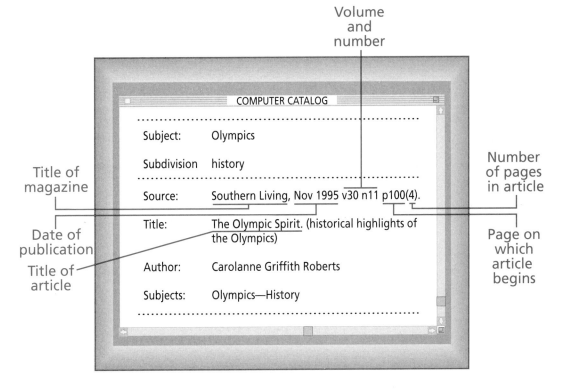

Activity G Study the sample entry above. Answer the following questions on your paper.

1) What is the name of the magazine shown on this computer screen?

2) How long is the article "The Olympic Spirit"?

3) Suppose you want to read the article. What issue of the magazine should you ask the librarian for?

4) Suppose you are researching the most recent Olympic records in swimming. Would this article be useful to you? Explain your answer.

You can also find magazine articles using the *Readers' Guide to Periodical Literature*. It is an index to articles in popular magazines.

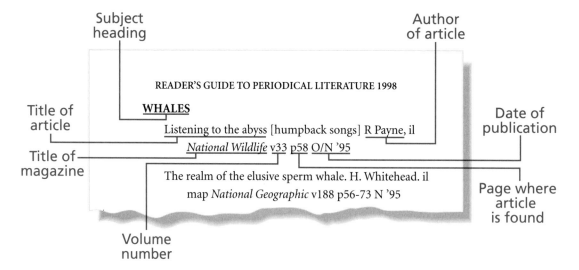

Activity H   Study the sample entries above. Answer the following questions on your paper.

1) Suppose you want to read the article in *National Geographic*. You should jot down a few items so that the librarian can help you find the article. What information from the *Readers' Guide* is most important to jot down?

2) In what issue of the magazine *National Wildlife* will you find an article about humpback whales?

Knowing What to Look Up

As you start researching your topic, list questions that you will try to answer in your report. Then think about how to find answers to your questions in books, reference sources, and periodicals. Use **key words** to find the information you need.

Key words

The words you look up to find information on a topic. They name what your question is about.

Suppose you are trying to answer this question: *How did Valentine's Day begin?* The key words in that question are *Valentine's Day*. You could look up those words in a library catalog. You could also look them up in an encyclopedia and in the index to a book about holidays.

Suppose this is your question: *What mammals are in danger of becoming extinct?* Key words might be *extinction* or *endangered animals*.

Activity I   Read each question below. Write what key word or key words would be likely to lead you to the answer.

1) What kinds of birds live in Hawaii?

2) Are any lizards poisonous?

3) What were the earliest computers like?

4) What are the rules for the game of lacrosse?

5) What languages are spoken in the Philippines?

Activity J   Write a list of questions for your own report topic. Then list key words that you think will be most useful in leading you to information.

Taking Notes

Think about your report topic and the questions you hope to answer. Make a list of main topics you can start searching for.

Mike is preparing a report on vegetable gardening. He has listed four possible main topics to include.

Report topic: Growing Vegetables

Main topics:

1. How to choose seeds

2. How to prepare the soil

3. When to plant each vegetable

4. When to harvest each vegetable

As Mike does his research, he may change some of his main topics. He will add subtopics. But his list will help him to take notes in an organized way.

Activity K Think about your own report topic. Write your own list of main topics to research.

Bibliography

A list of books and periodicals that have been used to find information.

Use one set of index cards to keep track of your sources. Use a separate card for each source. These cards will help you make a **bibliography**.

For a book, write the author's last name first. Underline the book title. Give the place of publication, the publisher, and the date of publication.

Sample bibliography card for book:

Jones, Robert C. *Your Vegetable Garden.*
New York: Tellmore Book Company,
1996.

For a magazine article, write the author's last name first. Use quotation marks around the title of the article. Underline the name of the magazine. Include the volume number, date, and page numbers.

Sample bibliography card for magazine article:

Ling, Marla. "Tips for City Gardeners".
Gardening Today 10 (May 5, 1995)
12–14.

Use a separate set of index cards for your notes. On each note card, list a main topic or subtopic. Then write information that fits with that topic. If you copy any exact words from your source, put quotation marks around them. On each note card, tell where you found the information.

Study these sample note cards. Notice how a main topic or subtopic is written at the top. Notice how the source is listed in a shortened form. The long form is on the bibliography card.

Choosing Seeds
Quality matters. "Home gardeners will reduce the chance of disappointment if they choose high quality seeds." (p. 81)
It's important to read the information on the packages.
Jones, p. 81

Garden Locations
People in cities can grow food. City gardeners can grow many vegetables in pots on windowsills and balconies.
Examples: tomatoes, radishes, herbs.
Ling, p. 12

Activity L Use Mike's cards above and on page 272 to answer these questions. Write your answers on your paper.

1) At the bottom of one of the note cards is *Jones, p. 81*. What does that mean?

2) Why has Mike written GARDEN LOCATIONS at the top of one of his note cards?

3) What did Robert C. Jones write?

4) In what magazine did Mike find Marla Ling's article?

5) Why did Mike put quotation marks around one of the sentences in his first note card?

Paraphrasing

As you take notes, use quotation marks around a writer's exact words. The other words in your notes should be your own. Instead of copying words and sentences, **paraphrase** the ideas you read about.

EXAMPLE

Author's Words: By the late twentieth century, some population experts were warning of dangers. They pointed to evidence that planet Earth no longer had the agricultural and energy resources to sustain its enormous human population.

Paraphrase: Scientists of the late twentieth century were studying population changes. Some warned that there were too many people in the world. Because food and fuel were running out, many lives were in danger.

Activity M   Paraphrase the information in these sentences. Rearrange ideas. Use synonyms. Add or delete words. Rewrite each sentence on your paper.

1) A gardener should buy seeds from expert growers except in special cases.

2) Seeds should be ordered well in advance of the planting season.

3) A gardener should order only the quantity of seeds needed for that growing season.

4) Most seeds now come in many varieties and can resist disease.

5) Some seeds live for as long as five years, but others are not good after only one year.

Activity N   Prepare to take notes on your report topic. Follow these steps.

1) Find a book or a magazine with information on your topic.

2) Prepare a bibliography card for that source.

3) Take notes on index cards. Write a main topic or a subtopic at the top of each card. If you copy words directly, put quotation marks around them. Paraphrase other information.

4) On the note card, write information about your source.

Find information for your report in an organized way.

- Use the library catalog to find books, magazines, and other reference books.
- Use index cards to keep track of your sources.
- Take notes on index cards. Each card should be labeled with a main topic or a subtopic.

Part A   Write your answer to each question in a complete sentence.

1) You want to find a book in the library catalog. What are three pieces of information you may use to look up the book?

2) You are writing a report about Albert Einstein. Should you look up *Albert* or *Einstein*?

3) Mike wants to find a book with information about turnips. He cannot find that subject in the library catalog. What should he do?

4) What reference book should you use to find out when the next leap year will be?

5) Where can you find information about an event that happened two months ago?

6) What kind of information does an atlas contain?

7) What are two kinds of periodicals?

8) You are writing a report about animal life in Alaska. You find a book called *Learning About Alaska*. How can you find out if this book has the information that you want?

9) Why are index cards often used for taking notes?

10) Why must you make a bibliography card for every source you use?

Part B   Continue researching your report topic. Remember to use bibliography cards. Remember to use note cards labeled with main topics and subtopics.

Outline

A list of information arranged by main topics and subtopics. An outline is a plan. An outline provides a framework for a report.

When you have finished finding information, you will have many note cards. Before you write your report, you must sort the note cards, or put them in order. Start by listing your main topics. Then choose an order to put them in. Finally, you will be able to write an **outline**. An outline will guide you in the writing of your report.

Here are the steps to follow in sorting your note cards.

1. Look at the topic or subtopic listed at the top of each card. Put the notes on the same topics together.

2. If you have only one card on a topic, see if it fits with one of the other topics.

3. If you have a large pile of cards on one topic, you may need to separate them into subtopics.

4. Some of your notes may not fit anywhere. You do not have to use all of the information that you found when you researched your topic.

Mike is writing a report about growing vegetables. He divided his note cards into five groups.

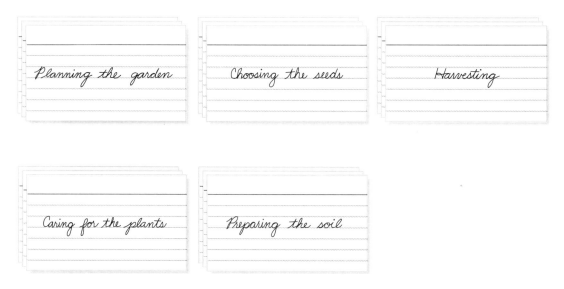

Planning the garden

Choosing the seeds

Harvesting

Caring for the plants

Preparing the soil

Activity A The bold word in each group below is the main topic. On your paper, write the subtopics that belong with this main topic. Ignore any subtopics that are not related to the main topic.

1) **Furniture:**   chair   table   window   sofa

2) **Books:**   magazine   dictionary   almanac   atlas

3) **Clothes:**   coat   hat   jewelry   shirt

4) **Sports:**   football   hockey   athlete   tennis

Activity B Look over the note cards you have been making for your own report. Sort the cards by main topics. Then write your own list of main topics for your report.

Choosing an Order

Think about the main topics you have listed for your report. How will you put the information into a logical order? There are many ways to organize the information. Choose the way that seems to fit your report topic best.

Several possible arrangements are listed below. Study the list.

Chronological order:	according to time, usually from the oldest to the most recent
Order of importance:	from the most to the least important or from the least to the most important
Order of size:	from the largest to the smallest or from the smallest to the largest
Order of cost:	from the most to the least expensive or from the least to the most expensive
Spatial order:	from left to right, top to bottom, or outside to inside
Other logical groupings:	first, second, third; easiest to hardest; least to most popular; least to most practical; and so on

Amanda is writing her term paper on early computers. How should she arrange her information? A logical way would be chronological order, the order in which events happened. She could start with the earliest computers and end with the invention of electronic computers.

Activity C   Read about the students' situations below. Each student must decide on an order for the main topics and subtopics in his or her report. Refer to the list of arrangements on page 277. Then write at least one way in which information could be arranged. In some cases, more than one logical order may be possible.

1) Mike's report is about growing vegetables. His main topics are planning the garden, choosing the seeds, caring for the plants, harvesting, and preparing the soil.

2) Shirley is investigating popular breeds of dogs in the United States. She has information about the five most popular breeds.

3) Laura is investigating firefighting methods. She has facts on several ways to put out a fire.

4) Derek has researched four energy sources of the future.

Activity D   Look over your list of main topics for your report. Decide on a logical arrangement for your information. Write what your arrangement is and why you think it will work.

Outlining

An outline is a kind of writer's guide. If you make an outline for your report, then you will know what to write first, next, and last. A good outline makes writing a report easier.

A topic outline lists only words and phrases. Outlines can also be written in complete sentences.

Mike has written the topic outline below. You should be able to see that Mike has chosen a chronologic order for his main topics.

- The main topics are listed after Roman numerals.

- The subtopics are indented and listed after capital letters.

- Further subtopics are indented and listed after Arabic numerals.

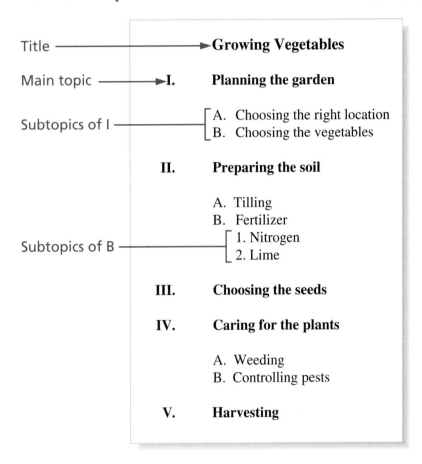

Title ——————————→ **Growing Vegetables**

Main topic ——————→ **I.** **Planning the garden**

Subtopics of I ————— A. Choosing the right location
B. Choosing the vegetables

II. **Preparing the soil**

A. Tilling
B. Fertilizer

Subtopics of B ————— 1. Nitrogen
2. Lime

III. **Choosing the seeds**

IV. **Caring for the plants**

A. Weeding
B. Controlling pests

V. **Harvesting**

Activity E On your paper, rewrite the outline above. Make each part a complete sentence.

Activity F Look at your own list of main topics for your report. Think about the order in which you plan to present them. Add subtopics to your list. Then write an outline for your report. Refer to the sample outline above as a guide.

Organize your notes. You will find that you are ready to begin writing your report.

- Sort your notes into groups of main topics and subtopics.
- Set aside the information that does not fit anywhere. You will not use it in your report.
- Arrange your main topics in a logical order. Refer to the list on page 277.
- Write a topic outline or a sentence outline. Refer to the example on page 279.

Part A Read this list of main topics for a report on the Olympic Games. Decide on a logical order in which the topics could be presented. List the topics in the order in which you would present them. Be ready to tell why you think your order is a good one.

Title: Olympic Games

Summer games

Famous Olympic athletes

How the games began

Winter games

The importance of the Olympics

Part B Read the list of topics and subtopics below. Rearrange them into a logical order. Then write a topic outline. Refer to the example on page 279 as a guide.

Title: Basic Car Care

The electrical system

The water pump

Engine lubrication

The radiator

The hoses

Battery

Replacing the oil filter

The cooling system

Changing engine oil

Spark plugs

Refer to your outline as you write your report. You will find that an outline makes the writing easier. Begin the report with a topic paragraph. Think of this paragraph as an introduction to your report. A topic paragraph tells your reader what the report will be about. Remember the three main parts of a paragraph:

- A *topic sentence* states the main idea.

- A *body* lists the main topics (I, II, III, and so on in your outline).

- A *summary sentence*.

Read the sample topic paragraph below. Compare the sentences in this paragraph to Mike's outline on page 279. Notice that the main topics are included. Subtopics will be discussed in the rest of the report.

Growing Vegetables

You can successfully grow vegetables in your own back yard. Five steps are involved. Begin by carefully planning the garden. Next, prepare the soil properly. Choose the best seed. During the growing season, give the plants the necessary care. Follow the detailed directions in this report to accomplish each of these steps. Harvest time will come much sooner than you may think!

Activity A   Write a topic paragraph to introduce a report on keeping in shape. Use the outline below. Write at least one sentence about each main topic.

Keeping in Shape

I.   Eating the right foods

II. Exercising daily

III. Getting proper rest

IV. Having a good attitude

Activity B   Write a topic paragraph for your own report. Write at least one sentence for each main topic from your outline. Try to make the topic of your report sound interesting to your readers.

Using Direct Quotations

Most of your report should be written in your own words. Sometimes it is effective to write the exact words of an author of one of your sources. When you were taking notes, you paraphrased most information. You used quotation marks around any words you copied. You jotted down the page where you found the quotation.

Study the example below. Notice how Mike has included a direct quotation in his paragraph. Notice the page number in parentheses. It tells where the quotation was found.

> Choosing the best seed for your garden is important. Scientists Robert Wiest and Augusta Low make this point: "Except in special cases, it pays the gardener to buy seeds from reputable nurseries and not to depend on home-grown supplies." (p. 24) They also advise gardeners to order seed well ahead of planting time.

Activity C   Read Mike's bibliography card and note card below. Then write the answers to the questions that follow.

Wiest, Robert, and Augusta Low. "Backyard Vegetables." <u>Natural Homes Magazine</u> 3 (January 1995) 24-28.

Preparing Soil

To have good soil you need organic matter — that's partly rotten plants. Leaves, lawn clippings, and straw will do. Gardeners should have a compost pile. "On some soils with naturally high fertility, only nitrogen or compost may be needed." (p. 25) Only add lime if tests show that it is needed.

Wiest & Low, p. 25

1) What was the source of Mike's information?

2) Was this information taken from a book or from a magazine?

3) Which sentence is a direct quotation? How can you tell?

4) From what page was this direct quotation copied?

Activity D   Write a paragraph about preparing soil. Paraphrase the information from the note card above. Use the direct quotation in your paragraph. Remember to indicate the source and to use quotation marks. Include the page number after the direct quotation.

Writing Summary Paragraphs

End your report with a summary paragraph. It repeats the main points of your report. A summary paragraph does not have to be long. It brings the report to a definite end.

Mike wrote this summary paragraph for his report. Notice how it sums up the main topics of his outline on page 279.

> Vegetables will grow even where there is limited space. If you want to see for yourself, just follow the steps that have been given in this report. Start by making a plan, preparing the soil, and choosing seeds. Caring for the plants can bring great satisfaction. Then you can have the satisfaction of plucking ripe vegetables. Finally, you will enjoy many delicious meals!

Activity E   Look back to the topic paragraph you wrote for Activity A. Think about the information that might have been included in the report "Keeping in Shape." Write a summary paragraph that could come at the end of that report.

Follow your outline, and you will write your report smoothly. Remember the three main parts of a report: the topic paragraph, the body, and the summary paragraph.

Part A Review your knowledge of reports. Write the letter of the correct answer for each question below.

1) When you put an author's information into your own words, what are you doing?
a) outlining   b) paraphrasing   c) reporting

2) What do you use as a guide when you write your report?
a) note cards   b) the title   c) an outline

3) Which part of the report is always more than one paragraph?
a) the topic sentence   b) the body   c) the summary

4) What is another name for the topic paragraph?
a) an introduction   b) an outline   c) a term paper

5) Why should you put quotation marks around an author's exact words?
a) to show that you have borrowed someone else's words
b) to show that you are paraphrasing
c) to show a bibliography

Part B Continue writing your report. You should have a collection of note cards, an outline, a title, and a topic paragraph. Take these remaining steps:

1) Write the body of your report. Write good paragraphs about the main topics and subtopics. Remember to include facts, details, examples, illustrations, and reasons. Use direct quotations (with page numbers) to emphasize important facts.

2) Make your last paragraph a summary of important points.

3) After you write your report, proofread it carefully. Revise it and rewrite it. Correct any mistakes.

4) Write the final report. Use a word processing program if possible. If you are handwriting, use ink.

The last step in writing a report or term paper is completing the bibliography. You have been using index cards to record information about each source. Your report will end with an alphabetic list of the sources you used.

Study the sample bibliography below. Notice the different forms used for a book, a periodical, and an encyclopedia. Here are two points to remember:

- If you are word processing, use italics for all titles of books or magazines. Otherwise, underline the titles.

- Use quotation marks around titles of articles in magazines or encyclopedias.

Bibliography

Allen, G., and M.K. Howard. *The History of Computers.* Chicago: Acme Books Co., 1996.

Brown, J.K., ed. *The Computer Encyclopedia.* New York: Computer Publications, Inc., 1995.

"Computer." *World Encyclopedia.* Vol. 3, 1996, 119–127.

"Computers of the Nineteenth Century." *Data World* 8 (March 1997) 54–57.

Evan, Stacey. "Computers Yesterday and Today." *The Computer Journal* 2 (August 1998) 9–11.

Activity A   Use the sample bibliography on page 286 to answer these questions.

1) Why is the book *The History of Computers* listed before *The Computer Encyclopedia?*

2) What information comes first in each entry?

3) Who wrote the article in *The Computer Journal?*

4) What does the abbreviation *ed.* mean?

5) Which two entries are periodicals?

6) In book entries, what punctuation mark is used after the place of publication?

7) If you were handwriting this bibliography, how would you show the title of a book or periodical?

8) What does the number 2 mean after the title *The Computer Journal?*

9) When was the book by Allen and Howard published?

10) Read carefully. What happens if the author is unknown?

Activity B   Study the sample bibliography entries on page 286. Then write the following entries in alphabetic order. Put each set of facts into the correct form. Be sure that your punctuation is correct.

Basic Car Care by Blakeley Richard. The book was published in Seattle by Automotive Publications in 1995.

"Fix It Yourself," an article by T. Ramirez in The Car Magazine, Volume 7, March 1999, on pages 67–72.

"Automobiles," in Universal Encyclopedia, Volume 1, 1995, on pages 144–152. No author is given.

The History of Automobiles, K.L. Lee, editor. The book was published in Boston by Cars and Company in 1996.

Activity C   Make a bibliography for your report. Start by getting your stack of bibliography cards. Then follow these steps.

1) Put your cards in alphabetic order according to the author's last name.

2) If there is no author, use the first important word of the title of the article or book.

3) Copy the information from each bibliography card to make a list.

4) Use the correct bibliographic form. Refer to the samples in this lesson on page 286.

The last pages of your report should be your bibliography. A bibliography is an alphabetic list of all the sources you used to write your report. Make sure to record all details about authors, titles, publishers, and dates. Use the correct form for each bibliographic entry.

Part A Read the five bibliographic entries below. Rewrite them in correct alphabetic order. Find the mistakes in each entry. Look for order, capitalization, and punctuation. Write each entry correctly.

Eating the right foods, A.L. Smith. Good Food Journal, May 1999, Volume 7, page 19.

Franklin, Sandra. Food and You. Nutrition Books, Inc., Chicago, 1997.

Gomez, C.V. The Right Kind of Exercise. NY, New York Book Co., 1998.

W.L. Fisher. Think Positive! 1998, Boston: Good Thoughts Press, Inc.

Young, J.F., ed. A Good Night to All. Carson City, NE: Carson City Press, 1996.

Part B Proofread the bibliography you wrote for your report. Revise it if you need to. Correct any mistakes.

Part A   Decide which topics listed below are included in this textbook, *Basic English Composition*. Use the table of contents and the index. If the topic is included, write *Yes*. If the topic is not included, write *No*.

1) Punctuating dialogue

2) Forms of irregular verbs

3) Using a dictionary

4) Topic sentences

5) Chronologic order

6) Footnotes

7) Outlines

8) Using telephone directories

9) Writing memos

10) Writing a summary

Part B   Read each question below. For each one, name the key words you would look up to find the answer. Tell what source you would use to find the answer.

1) What is the dance called the waltz?

2) Where is the Asian country of Myanmar?

3) When were motorcycles invented?

4) Can peaches be grown in a cold climate?

5) How big was the first electronic computer?

6) Are crows and blue jays related?

7) Where did basketball begin?

8) What is the record for running the mile?

9) Who was Marian Anderson?

10) Who was the president of the United States after Abraham Lincoln?

Part C   Read these sentences of information. Paraphrase each one. Write the same information in your own words.

1) With a lifetime batting average of .317, Pittsburgh Pirates outfielder Roberto Clemente was an outstanding baseball player.

2) Nicaragua is the largest nation in Central America.

3) The animal known as the big brown bat is actually only about four inches long.

4) Hurricanes are damaging storms often accompanied by rain and high tides.

5) Whatever is stored in a computer's RAM (Random Access Memory) is lost when the computer is turned off.

Part D   Make a neat, final copy of your own report. Make a title page.

> The History of Computers
> Amanda O'Hara
> June 9, 1998

Assemble the report in this order:

1. Title page   **3.** Bibliography

2. Report   **4.** Blank page at end

Your goal was to write a well-organized, fact-filled, interesting report. How well do you think you reached your goal? Write a few sentences to answer that question.

Test Taking Tip   Study any examples that follow a set of directions in a test. Make sure you understand why the example is done as shown. If the example is not clear to you, read the directions again.

Glossary

A

Action verb—(ak´shən vėrb) a word that expresses action in a sentence; it tells what someone or something does: *Throw* the ball. They *run* fast. Please *think* of an answer. (p. 50)

Adjective—(aj´ ik tiv) a word that describes a noun or pronoun; it tells how many, what kind, or which one (p. 47)

Adverb—(ad´ vėrb) a word that answers questions about a verb, an adjective, or another adverb; it tells *when, how, how often, where,* or *to what degree* (p. 135)

Agreement—(ə grē´ mənt) the logical match between two elements of a sentence (p. 32)

Anecdote—(an´ ik dōt) a very short story about an interesting or amusing happening (p. 194)

Antecedent—(an tə sēd´ nt) the noun to which a pronoun refers (p. 40)

Apostrophe—(ə pos´ trə fē) a punctuation mark used to replace missing letters in a contraction (*doesn't*) or to show possession (*Mary's* coat) (p. 65)

B

Bibliography—(bib lē og´ rə fē) a list of books and periodicals that have been used to find information (p. 272)

Body—(bod´ ē) the part of a paragraph that discusses the main idea; these sentences can include reasons, facts, examples, or illustrations (p. 169)

Business letter—(biz´ nis let´ ər) a formal message written to a person or an organization (p. 249)

C

Capital letter—(kap´ ə təl let´ ər) the uppercase form of a letter: *A, B, C,* and so on (p. 2)

Case—(kās) the form of a noun or pronoun that tells its relation to other words in a sentence (p. 43)

Catalog—(kat´ l og) a list of items arranged in a special way (p. 262)

Chronological order—(kron ə loj´ ə kəl ôr´ dər) arrangement according to time, usually from oldest to most recent (p. 196)

Command—(kə mand´) a sentence that tells or orders someone to do something (p. 12)

Common noun—(kom´ ən noun) the general name of a person, place, thing, or idea; it begins with a lowercase letter: *child, playground, swing, happiness* (p. 47)

Comparative form—(kəm par´ ə tiv fôrm) the form of an adjective or adverb used to compare two people, places, things, or actions; it is formed by adding *-er* to the base word or by using the word *more* or *less*: small, *smaller;* quickly, *more quickly, less quickly* (p. 138)

Compare—(kəm pâr´) to point out ways in which two or more things are alike or different (p. 211)

Comparison—(kəm pâr´ ə sən) a statement about how two or more things are alike or different (p. 211)

Compound subject—(kom´ pound sub´ jikt) two subjects joined by *and* (p. 38)

Conclusion—(kən klü´ zhən) a logical judgment based on evidence; often presented at the end of a paragraph or an essay (p. 173)

Conjunction—(ken jungk´ shən) a word used to connect words or phrases or to combine complete ideas in sentences: *and, or, but* (p. 118)

Consistent—(kən sis´ tənt) following the same rules; staying the same (p. 53)

Contraction—(kən trak´ shən) a shortened form of one or two words; an apostrophe stands for the missing letters: *they're, he'll, jumpin'* (p. 86)

D

Dependent clause—(di pen´ dənt klȯz) a group of related words that contains a subject and a verb but that does not express a complete idea (*Before the phone rang*) (p. 156)

Dialogue—(dī´ ə lȯg) the words that people or story characters say to each other (p. 17)

Direct comparison—(də rekt´ kəm par´ ə sən) an expression showing that two things have similar qualities; also called a *metaphor* (p. 212)

Direct quotation—(də rekt´ kwō tā´ shən) sentences reporting the exact words that someone said; quotation marks enclose these exact words (p. 22)

Discuss—(dis kus´) to tell about; a discussion should include the good and the bad characteristics of a topic; a discussion may include the writer's opinion about the topic (p. 225)

E

End punctuation mark—(end pungk chü ā´ shən märk) a mark that comes at the end of a sentence and tells the reader where the complete idea ends; the three end punctuation marks are: *period (.), question mark (?),* and *exclamation mark (!)* (p. 2)

Essay—(es´ ā) a short piece of writing about a single subject or topic (p. 223)

Exaggerate—(eg zaj´ ə rāt) to overstate; to say that something is greater than it is (p. 213)

Exclamation—(ek sklə mā´ shən) an expression of strong feeling (p. 12)

F

Feminine pronoun—(fem´ ə nen prō´ noun) a word that replaces a noun naming a female person; the feminine pronouns are *she, her, hers, herself* (p. 42)

Fiction—(fik´ shən) an imaginary story; writing based largely on the writer's imagination (p. 194)

Fragment—(frag´ mənt) a group of words that does not express a complete thought; a phrase or clause incorrectly treated as a sentence (p. 122)

G

Gender—(jen´ dər) the characteristic of nouns and pronouns that tells they are masculine *(man, he)*, feminine *(woman, she)*, or neuter *(puppy, it)* (p. 42)

H

Helping verb—(hel´ ping vėrb) a verb form that helps main verbs to express time: We *must* go. I *have* cooked. Laura *will* see us. The dog *has been* eating. (p. 50)

Homonyms—(hom´ ə nimz) words that sound alike but have different meanings and spellings (p. 74)

I

Identify—(ī den´ tə fī) to tell the most important characteristics of something; these characteristics make the person, place, or thing different or recognizable (p. 221)

Independent clause—(in də pen´ dənt klöz) a group of words that includes a subject and a verb; it may be written alone as a complete sentence, or it may be combined with another clause (p. 155)

Index—(in´ deks) an alphabetic list of all topics and subtopics in a book; each listing is followed by the numbers of pages on which information is found (p. 267)

Indirect comparison—(in də rekt´ kəm pâr´ ə sən) an expression using *like* or *as* to show that things are like each other in a certain way; also called a *simile* (p. 212)

Indirect quotation—(in də rekt´ kwō tā´ shən) sentences that report what someone said without using the speaker's exact words (p. 22)

Investigate—(in ves´ tə gāt) to search thoroughly; to examine (p. 264)

Irregular plural noun—(i reg´ yə lər plür´ əl noun) a noun that forms its plural in an unusual way, not with the usual *-s* or *-es*: mouse, *mice*; foot, *feet*; man, *men* (p. 66)

Irregular verb—(i reg´ yə lər vėrb) a verb that does not form its past and past participle by adding *-ed* to the present tense form: *eat, ate, eaten* (p. 56)

K

Key words—(kē wėrdz) the words you look up to find information on a topic; they name what your question is about (p. 270)

M

Masculine pronoun—(mas´ kyə lin prō´ noun) a word that replaces a noun naming a male person; the masculine pronouns are *he, him, his, himself* (p. 42)

Memorandum—(mem ə ran´ dəm) an informal message written in special form and frequently used in the business world; often shortened to *memo* (p. 235)

a	hat	e	let	ī	ice	ô	order	ù	put	sh	she	ə	a	in about
ā	age	ē	equal	o	hot	oi	oil	ü	rule	th	thin		e	in taken
ä	far	ėr	term	ō	open	ou	out	ch	child	ᵺ	then		i	in pencil
â	care	i	it	ò	saw	u	cup	ng	long	zh	measure		o	in lemon
													u	in circus

Message—(mes´ij) communication, either written or spoken (p. 232)

Metaphor—(met´ə fôr) see *Direct comparison* (p. 212)

Modifier—(mod´ə fī ər) a word that describes another word in a sentence (p. 132)

N

Neuter pronoun—(nü´tər prō´noun) a word that replaces the name of any place, thing, or idea in a sentence; neuter singular pronouns are *it, its, itself* (p. 42)

Nominative case—(nom´ə nə tiv kās) the form of a pronoun that shows it is being used as a subject: *I* sing; *he* dances; *we* perform (p. 43)

Nonfiction—(non fik´shən) writing that expresses facts and ideas; a true story, rather than an imaginary one (p. 194)

Noun—(noun) the name of a person, place, thing, or idea: *teacher, museum, ball, heroism* (p. 32)

Number—(num´bər) the characteristic of a noun or pronoun that tells whether it is singular or plural (p. 43)

O

Objective case—(ab jek´tiv kās) the form of a pronoun that shows it is being used as an object: sing with *me*; hold *him*; perform for *us* (p. 43)

Outline—(out´līn) a list of information arranged by main topics and subtopics; an outline is a plan; an outline provides a framework for a report (p. 276)

P

Paragraph—(par´ə graf) a group of sentences about one idea or topic; it usually has three parts: a topic sentence or introduction, a body, and a conclusion or summary (p. 164)

Paraphrase—(par´ə frāz) to express someone else's ideas in your own words (p. 274)

Past participle—(past pär´tə sip əl) a principal part of a verb, used to form the perfect tenses (p. 55)

Periodicals—(pir ē od´ə kəlz) any printed materials published at regular intervals; magazines and newspapers (p. 269)

Personal letter—(pėr´sə nəl let´ər) an informal message written to a friend or a relative (p. 242)

Personal narrative—(pėr´sə nəl nar´ə tiv) a true story told from the viewpoint of the narrator (p. 194)

Persuade—(pər swād´) to write or talk in a convincing way; to give reasons and facts that convince others to act or believe in a certain way; to appeal to feelings in order to convince (p. 191)

Phrase—(frāz) a group of words that does not contain a subject or predicate, such as a prepositional phrase or a verb phrase (p. 144)

Plural—(plùr´əl) referring to more than one person, place, or thing: *houses, nations, doctors, they* (p. 32)

Point of view—(point ov vyü) an opinion; the way in which something is looked at (p. 203)

Positive form—(poz´ə tiv fôrm) the basic form of an adjective or adverb; it makes no comparison (p. 138)

Possessive case—(pə zes´iv kās) the form of a pronoun that shows ownership or relationship: The song is *mine*; hold *his* hand; watch *our* performance (p. 43)

Possessive noun—(pə zes´iv noun) a noun that names the owner of something or names a relationship between people or things; a possessive noun must have an apostrophe: *Mary's* coat; the *woman's* car; the *voters'* opinions (p. 65)

Predicate—(pred´ə kit) the part of a sentence that tells something about the subject; it always contains a verb (p. 123)

Prepositional phrase—(prep ə zish´ə nəl frāz) a group of words made up of a preposition and its object; it may be used as either an adjective or an adverb *(to the store, by the road)* (p. 144)

Pronoun—(prō´noun) a word used in place of a noun (p. 34)

Proofread—(prüf´rēd) to look for mistakes in spelling, grammar, punctuation, and other things (p. 185)

Proper adjective—(prop´ər aj´ik tiv) a describing word formed from a proper noun: *French food* (p. 47)

Proper noun—(prop´ər noun) the name of a particular person, place, thing, or idea; it begins with a capital letter: *Frances, Osgood Park, U.S. Senate, Stone Age* (p. 47)

Q

Question—(kwes´chən) a sentence that asks for information (p. 12)

Quotation—(kwō tā´ shən) a passage containing someone's exact spoken or written words; the words are enclosed in quotation marks (" ") (p. 17)

Report—(ri pôrt´) an organized summary of information about a topic that has been researched; a report may be written or spoken (p. 260)

Request—(ri kwest´) a mild command; it politely tells someone to do something; it often includes the word *please* (p. 12)

Research—(rē´ sėrch) to look for information about a topic by reading books and periodicals, by observing events, or by questioning experts (p. 264)

Revise—(ri vīz´) to correct errors or to make changes (p. 185)

Rewrite—(rē rīt´) to write again (p. 185)

Run-on sentence—(run on sen´ təns) two or more complete ideas that are not connected correctly: *I have read that book many times I'll read it again, it is my favorite and you'll like it too.* (p. 116)

Sentence—(sen´ təns) a group of words containing a subject and a verb and expressing a complete idea (p. 2)

Simile—(sim´ ə lē) see *Indirect comparison* (p. 212)

Singular—(sing´ gyə lər) referring to one person, place, or thing: *house, nation, doctor, it* (p. 32)

Statement—(stāt´ mənt) a sentence that expresses a fact or gives information (p. 12)

State-of-being verb—(stāt ov bē´ ing vėrb) a word that expresses the condition of the subject; it connects the subject with a noun, pronoun, or adjective: Richard *is* my brother. The woman *looks* tired. (p. 50)

Subject—(sub´ jikt) the person, place, or thing that the sentence tells about: *Donald ate a sandwich.* (subject: *Donald*) (p. 32)

Subordinating conjunction—(sə bôrd´ n āt´ ing kən jungk´ shən) a conjunction that joins a dependent clause to an independent clause *(because, when, since)* (p. 156)

Subtopic—(sub´ top ik) a division or a part of a larger topic: *Video games* is one subtopic under the main topic *Computers* (p. 261)

Summary—(sum´ ər ē) a statement that briefly repeats main points, often as the last sentence of a paragraph or the last sentences of an essay (p. 173)

Superlative form—(sə pėr´ lə tiv fôrm) the form of an adjective or adverb used to compare more than two people, places, things, or actions; it is formed by adding *-est* to the base word or by using the word *most* or *least*: small, *smallest*; quickly, *most quickly*, *least quickly* (p. 138)

Synonyms—(sin´ ə nimz) words that have a similar meaning: *big* and *large; happy* and *glad* (p. 134)

Table of contents—(tā´ bəl ov kon´ tents) a list of the parts of a book and the page on which each part begins (p. 267)

Tense—(tens) the form of a verb that expresses time (p. 52)

Term paper—(tėrm pā´ pər) a formal report in which a writer tries to prove a thesis or an idea about a chosen topic (p. 260)

Thesaurus—(thi sôr´ əs) a reference source that lists words and their synonyms (p. 134)

Topic sentence—(top´ ik sen´ təns) a sentence that states the main idea in a paragraph; it is often the first sentence (p. 164)

Transition—(tran zish´ ən) an expression that connects ideas, sentences, or paragraphs *(however, therefore, on the other hand, in the meantime)* (p. 208)

Variety—(və rī´ ə tē) a number or collection of many different things (p. 205)

Verb—(vėrb) a word used to express action or state of being: *Donald ate a sandwich.* (action verb: *ate*) *Donald was hungry.* (state-of-being verb: *was*) (p. 32)

Verb phrase—(vėrb frāz) a group of words including a main verb and any helping verbs (p. 50)

a	hat	e	let	ī	ice	ȯ	order	u̇	put	sh	she		a	in about
ā	age	ē	equal	o	hot	oi	oil	ü	rule	th	thin	ə	e	in taken
ä	far	ėr	term	ō	open	ou	out	ch	child	ᵗͪ	then		i	in pencil
â	care	i	it	ȯ	saw	u	cup	ng	long	zh	measure		o	in lemon
													u	in circus

Index

relevant information, 264–75
taking notes, 271–73
Return address
on business letter, 249
on personal letter envelope, 245
Revise/rewrite
addresses, 256
business letters, 257
defined, 185
essay answers, 227
memos, 236–37
messages, 233
outline, 279
reports, 285
sentences, 205–07
topic sentences, 202–04
Run-on sentence, 116–21

S

Salutation
business letter, 249
personal letter, 242
Sentence fragments, 122–27
Sentences, 1–9
agreement of subject and verb in, 32–39
beginning and ending, 2–4
capitalization in, 2–7, 47–49
complete, for short answers, 220
connections and combinations of, 151–59
defined, 2
fragments of, 122–27
in letters, 241–57
making each count, 131–61
in paragraphs, 163–77, 179–99, 201–17
possessives and plurals in, 65–69
predicate of, 123
pronouns in, 40–46
punctuating, 2–7, 11–29
purpose of, 12–16
in report, 259–91
run-on, 116–21
spelling counts in, 73–113
subject of, 123
supporting paragraph idea, 170–71
topic, 164–68
in essay answers, 223–24
variety in, 205–07
verbs in, 50–64
word order in, 3
writing, 25–27
complete, 115–29
correct, 31–71
dialogue with, 17–24

Short answers, 220–22
Signature
on business letter, 249
on personal letter, 242
Simile, 212. *See also* Indirect comparison
Singular, 32
Singular noun, 32
apostrophe with, 66
neuter pronouns and, 42
plural form of, 91–95
Singular personal pronouns, 44
Singular pronoun, 34–35
Singular verbs, 32
Spelling
of almost-alike words, 81–85
of contractions and possessive pronouns, 86–90
of difficult words, 109–11
importance of, 73–113
of plural nouns, 91–98
of sound-alike words, 74–80
of words with endings, 102–08
of words with *ie* or *ei,* 99–101
Spelling demons, 109–11
Statement, 12
State-of-being verb
adjective following, 133
defined, 50
Stationery, 249
Story
chronological order in, 196
dialogue in, 195
sentences in, 25–26
telling a, 194–97
Subject
agreement of verb and, 32–39
compound, 38
defined, 32
finding the, 37
singular, 32
Subordinating conjunction, 156–58
Subtopic, 261
Summary
defined, 173
in essay answer, 223
paragraph, 284
Superlative form
defined, 138
irregular, 141
Synonyms, 134